Leader Champions: Secrets Of Success

by

Mark B. Silber, Ph.D.
And
Antonio F. Vianna, M.M.

First published by AuthorHouse 05/08/04

ISBN: 1-4184-5651-9 (e-book)
ISBN: 1-4184-3685-2 (Paperback)
ISBN: 1-4184-3684-4 (Dust Jacket)

Library of Congress Control Number: 2004092219

Printed in the United States of America
Bloomington, IN

This book is printed on acid free paper.

L eadership is a learned skill,
and an art. It includes
sensitivity and the personal
strength to unify a diverse
group of talented people to
effectively work together to
achieve meaningful and personally
owned goals with a set of shared values.

The Leader Champion is one
who actively promotes this cause,
and is prepared to withstand adversity.

Mark B. Silber, Ph.D.
Antonio F. Vianna, M. M.

DEDICATIONS

Here is to the years of my life
The years of enjoyment & caring
The years with my wife
The years of love and laughing
With
My very dear Elizabeth.
Mark B. Silber

With forever love to Paula,
who taught me the lessons
of human compassion and caring;
to Felix,
who nurtured in the lessons of persistence;
to Victoria,
who is always at my side
during my life's experiences.
Antonio F. Vianna

ACKNOWLEDGMENTS

For supportive contribution of this book, we thank Ms. Kathy Pennington and Ms. Jean Caswell. For content guidance and professional feedback, we thank Marge Silber. Kudos and recognition for legal assistance and uplifting emotional stimulation to Jerome H. Silber.

Table of Contents

Preface

Complexity is a manager's conflicting push-pull world, often in opposing directions. There is the informal political world of the organizational culture that breeds dangerous competitions for position survival and second-guessing. There are the changing legal and shifting environmental requirements that must be adhered to, to prevent personal punishment, organizational fines and court-assigned penalties. It is no wonder that today's manager asks, "Who's on first?"

Twenty-first Century personnel downsizing at all levels because of economic pressures from overseas companies add to this tangled complexity. Outsourcing of customer service centers, outsourcing of major manufacturing operations, transfers of total product production capabilities, and even Research and Development talent being re-located overseas, produce anger and resentment in the manager's unsettling world.

Employee and social values have changed! What are not socially and politically correct expressions and behaviors add to managerial complexity. Ever increasing sophistication of employees at all levels add to the manager's conundrum. Their university-based training in business administration schools does not work. Managers today have become a target of employees' changing expectations. Many befuddled companies wonder what they must do to regain employee loyalty and trust.

Television, newspapers, business magazines highlight executive ethical decay and immoral business manipulations. The confusion of ethics versus economics, the conflicts of money versus moral mission are symptomatic of managing today. These symptoms are in search for both curative answers and pain relief. The lot of the manager is not a peaceful lot today.

Continuous changes, Human Resources shifting complexities, and information overload call for an applied and practical book, a non-academic textbook to assist managers and managers-to-be in their quest to deal effectively with their multi-tasking roles. Some want to be a Leader Champion. This action-oriented book is a insightful look at the 21st Century manager and how to succeed in her/his dynamic relationships and responsibilities. This is the real world of behaviors for results.

Going beyond the insights of leadership, this practical book answers some of the questions of why organizations falter and fail, why many of yesterday's companies became the house of the living dead without vitality or zest.

Albeit a modest leadership look at organizational systems, this book explores how to increase operations' excellence. What seems to separate systems that just work from operational systems that maintain vitality and meet the changing needs of competition? How and why do organizational systems become rocks and blocks to fast-paced achieving? If blame is to be focused, might it be focused on outdated operational system constrictions, outdated systems that use to work in the past but no longer hold value today?

Here is a hard-hitting and easy to read book that has the following no-nonsense performance objectives:

To facilitate those person's climb who wish to move up the corporate ladder, to be the Leader Champion, by identifying many tips for career success that are based on some unique and effective managerial techniques. What seems to undergird the positive impact of the emerging leader's successful career progression and executive career ascent?

To increase the reader's awareness of the Human Resources sensitivities needed to gain political visibility, personal effectiveness, managing excellence and follower acceptance within the dynamics of the organization. This directly deals with increasing human relations skills and goal accomplishments. Employees' contemporary values and changing employee expectations are central to many of the following pages. This is the human side of the management profession.

To assist the executive practitioner, the management educator, the Business Administration Professor and the in-field organizational consultant with vivid examples of performance and operational excellence to use as benchmarks. Organizational living is central to the reading of this tough-minded section.

To provide a hands-on text that focuses on personal management improvement, and stimulates managerial skill building that addresses human relations competence and suggests how to increase the meaningfulness of organizational systems. It is a how-to book designed to stimulate managerial skill building as well as executive performance capability within organizational systems of getting a job done.

To offer alternatives from traditional Organizational Psychology that managers might consider when facing 21st Century conflicts. These anxieties appear when faced in their push-pull world and the global-village competitive pressures. Specifically, this text offers practical insights for results, and addresses many of the issues sometimes hidden in the fog of corporate living and career enhancement. We offer a book for winners, about winning ways, for the Leader Champion!

This book was explicitly designed and written for use: (1) in both graduate and undergraduate business school curricula, (2) by those individuals who are committed to their upward executive career climb, and (3) those to-be manager aspirants who wish to explore the real world of the management profession, aspirants who are not sure if management is for them. It was written with the goals of being relevant, practical, clear easy readability and thought-provoking insights.

It is our fervent hope that this up to date, pace-setting book meaningfully assists the personal growth of aspiring and present members of management as they go about their praiseworthy profession: the profession of getting action results, the profession of handling human relationships, the profession of management.

It is our belief that only with improving managers will the organization improve. An organization so often starts to die and decay with inept managing, insensitive administrators, and rigid outdated systems.

Operations, which no longer contribute to the excellence of the corporation, are the death rattle of that dying organization.

The motivated focus of (1) personal and (2) corporate excellence are needed bed partners. The vitality of change is the vitality of competitive growth. There is a saying, "Death is God's way of telling you to slow down!" Unfortunately, the days of the slow repetitive pace are days gone by! The with-it executive is analytical and decisive in order to anticipate and meet the competitive challenges.

This book is about realistic Leader Champion skills. It is about experiencing, judging, evaluating, and adapting. It is about your choices for the 21st Century.

This book can be about YOU.

It is YOUR choice.

Definitions

MANAGEMENT CAREER: IS IT FOR YOU?

Do you know your Interests, Skills, Motivation, and Capacity to be a manager? Do you know what organizational culture is best suited for your success? Do you have the emotional, intellectual, and physical stamina to be a manager? What risks are you willing to take while adhering to your personal code of ethics to succeed? Career ascent is partially built on your political connections and your mentors. Build these political-learning connections slowly and with diligence/graciousness. Fitting-in successfully in an organization requires healthy and positive interfaces with all levels of higher management.

LEADERSHIP.

The key to leadership, getting things done through other people who might not be willing to do it by themselves, is in strategically leveraging the value of people. If people are an organization's greatest asset, then it seems that maximizing the people asset has both economic and strategic consequences for the organization and for the person. Identifying, maximizing, measuring, and reporting on the people value is an opportunity for the leader.

PRACTICAL POINTERS OF MANAGING FOR RESULTS.

When all is said-and-done, methods and achievements of agreed upon results are the combined bottom line. Result by any means is not the answer. Men and women become leader champions. They are not born winners, pre-destined for the winner's circle. This Section offers practical time and priority management methods. Leader champion managers persuade, negotiate, and influence positive change in ethical ways. Some secrets of survival in the organizational political

1

jungle include the importance of having an organizational sponsor and an ongoing relationship with a mentor to guide and protect you as you take decision-making risks. Risk-taking is the bed partner of decision making.

HUMAN RELATIONS.

Develop trust with others, a belief that you will do what you say you will do so others can depend on you; develop harmonious working relationships with a diverse group of stakeholders.

INTERPERSONAL SKILLS.

The core of relations is sensitivity to others' mindsets and discovering the needs of others. It is an evolving process of the growth of trust between and among persons. Trust is earned based on honesty, openness and the focused, active listening to understand others. It is the alertness of sincerely being mutually interested in each other's qualities.

PERSONNEL MATTERS.

Be objective and fair, demonstrate ways to help others gain success; follow established legal and organizational protocols; encourage a positive uplifting environment.

SENSITIVITIES.

Be observant about how others react to you, and respect the dignity and values of others without compromising your own belief system; stop behavior from others that undermine positive feelings and relationships.

Success: Personal Living Effectiveness

The trilogy of an individual's present and future career is (1) job life visibility of being both efficient and effective, (2) leadership poise, political stance, bearing and skills, and (3) well being in living one's personal life. Personal reputation of having a well rounded life of socialization, known behavior of demonstrated ethics and having a healthy mind and body in handling life's highs and lows of stress are major components of personal living effectiveness. Self-insight and self-awareness is a perquisite for your beginning.

PRACTICAL MANAGEMENT IDEAS.

The two major objectives of management are (1) P= motivational impact on PEOPLE and (2) P= increasing PERFORMANCE PRODUCTIVITY. The core component of both "P's" is influencing negotiated changes. Changes are facilitated

2

when people take motivational ownership of meaningful tasks through the utilization and growth of their talents. Productivity changes succeed as managers communicate clear targets of performance expectations based on tough-minded decision making.

MOTIVATION.

One of the many tightly held secrets of leadership is how to align the employee's identification of him/herself, to his/her profession, to the job and to the organization. How can the leader gain the employee's emotional passion and ownership of their assignments? While many leaders have insight into building team commitment, motivating the employee is something different. Leader champions encourage the multi-layered attitude by working with employees and by stimulating the release of their internal motivation that is already within them.

TEAMS.

21st Century organizations have made a proactive commitment to teaming. This means these high performance enterprises lead through team and effective group interaction. The eras of rugged individualism are less acceptable now. Being an active member of an integrated team, a member who has sensitivity, and who honestly contributes to enriching the total team results, is key to contemporary organizational life.

SYSTEMS, OPERATIONS, and STRUCTURE.

A key to success in organizational life is the ability to scan the environment for deficiencies and efficiencies, knowing what to add, delete, reinforce, and tweak. All organizations are not created equal. Each is unique.

Management Career: Is It for You?

Management Career: Is It for You?

Career ascent is partially built on your political connections and your mentors. Build these political-learning connections slowly and with diligence/ graciousness. Fitting-in successfully in an organization requires healthy and positive interfaces with all levels of higher management. Your performance does need organizational visibility.

Leadership is not a position, but both relationships and action. Leadership is not a popularity contest. You are bound to be disliked at times.

Climbing to ever higher leader levels of peak performance is like brushing your teeth. You need to do it every day. If your future is to be better than your present, your future must be paid for by today's peak performance and today's new learning. Be a learner, not a leaner.

Awareness of a need to change, to attenuate, or to stop doing something is a sign of a mature leader champion.

As a leader champion, do not try to be everything to everybody. Do not spread yourself too thin. What are you going to give up today to be a winner tomorrow? If you are unwilling to give up things and pay the price, then be happy with being unsuccessful. You must constantly invest in your future. Willingness to self-examine and to self-explore the cause/s of problems helps the leader champion handle the 'rough sea changes.'

Senior Management Dreams.

The higher you climb on the management ladder, the more your anatomy shows. Are you truly willing to be more of a target? Higher management is not for everyone. Being a leader champion means you must change from being a competitor to a cooperator.

Leadership

Leadership

A key to leadership, getting things done through other people who might not be willing to do it by themselves, is in strategically leveraging the value of people. At face value, as people are an organization's greatest asset, then it seems to reason that maximizing the people asset has both economic and positive consequences for the organization and for the person. Identifying, maximizing, measuring, and reporting on the people value is an opportunity for the leader.

If you can not influence, persuade, negotiate with skill and sensitivity in an organization, you do not lead.

Know when to say 'No.' Establish and keep priorities. Give up time wasters. Stay focused and disciplined on targets.

The real goal of a leader is not to make people feel good, but rather to facilitate in letting them be good, to be great, and to grow.

The positive aspect of organizational conflict is to negotiate what is fair and what is just. These goals must be hammered out and negotiated in win - win outcomes.

It is perfectly acceptable to be controversial. At the same time, be considerate and other-person concerned during the persuasion encounter. Let the other person out talk you if that is what it takes for mutual gain.

Ethics is about right and wrong. Do you know what your ethical philosophy is and how you demonstrate it to others? Sometimes you feel it in your stomach. Be careful of instincts and reactive gut feelings. They are only signs to alert. Critically ask yourself what the feelings mean.

Accept what cannot be changed from what can be changed. Influence what is within your arena of control.

You Can Not Control Everything.

Be emotionally willing to let go. Pull by your vision and mission, not push for control over others. When you try too hard to prove your adequacy and expertise, you might prove your inadequacy and incompetence.

Up The Corporate Ladder.

Career climbing seems to relate to those individuals who have "psychological ants in their mental pants." They are conservatively restless individuals who want to get on with it. They ask themselves how they can be more effective. This is an action attitude. If you are going to climb a mountain, you need to start moving yourself before trying to move the organizational mountain.

Taking Charge of a Department.

As you take over a group or department, critically think about your management approaches. Think about being the manager you wish you had in your past. Your past positive role models may work wonders for you. Winners mirror the winners they had in the past, and they remember the short comings of poor past managers.

Be a player, not an observer.
Do not casually play at leadership.
Be an action player,
rather than
a managerial pass-over.

When confronted with decision dilemmas, seek to fully consider the beliefs of others and the relationship you have with them as you attempt to gain the best possible outcome for all stakeholders.

Leadership and Managementship.

There can be a co-mingling of the art of leadership with the practical skills of management:

Good leadership with good management means a great place to work.

Good leadership with bad management leads to disorganization.

Bad leadership with good management keeps things moving along.

Bad leadership with bad management sinks the ship.

A leader champion is a dream doer, not just a dreamer of what might be, ought to be, or could be. A leader champion is a realist of what is and what is not. A leader champion is not a self-deceiver.

A leader champion juggles multiple balls in the air, knowing full well their inability to be everything to everybody at all times. They deal with and face many things sequentially, but not simultaneously. They invest and utilize time, neither spending nor passing time, for it is too precious to waste.

Leader champions are divergent thinkers. Their thinking pattern proceeds in an expanding and open manner under stress, absorbing the threat of danger. Their thinking does not contract on small details, getting wrapped up in the trivia. They explore options, rather than embrace the first or only one perceived solution to a complex problem.

Leader champions take the time to think about targets. They get away from their executive desk to identify where there are significant opportunities to commit focused attention and staff effort. They do not tinker and linger with yesterday's problems.

Within a department or division, there are informal group leaders who hold no formal power of position or authority. These persons can be your friend or foe. Seek out informal leaders to be your friends.

Be a lamplighter and light up the performance light of others so that they can be seen by others. Do not cover or hide the achievements of your staff. Keep the light beam on them, not you. As others' lights burn brightly, leaders look good in their glow.

Different Folks Need Different Strokes.

Leaders are full of awe of others. The leader champion must learn to treat and
utilize different employees differently. There is no one best way to lead everyone.
Although differences exist between and among staff members,
a constant is each person's need for recognition and attention. Differences are just
differences; not one person better or less than another person.

Good and bad gossip is a real part of organizational existence.
Learn to carefully listen to gossip,
but do not repeat it.

One of the most difficult personal challenges might be to ask someone for a
second chance, with the desire to be recognized for changed behavior.

M-I-L-E-S Markers of Leader Behavior.

Mentally visualize outcomes and coming positive attractions.

Imagine the sub-step actions needed for final results.

Live and face the present realities that are to be confronted.

Enthusiastically expect to succeed.

Stop worrying about making decisions; make them to the best of your ability.

Mark B. Silber, Ph.D. And Antonio F. Vianna, M.M.

Reputation and Privacy.

Part of a leader's valuable reputation,
a reputation that precedes you in an organization, is your discreteness in handling
private and privileged information. Discreteness is as valuable as the reputation
for confidentiality.

Face Time.

Face time is walking and talking with and among everyone.
Computer e-mails and bulletin board messages must never replace
face time familiarity.
There are many reward currencies, beyond financial rewards,
that can be given to others.
The richest currency that people can take to their emotional bank is the feeling
that their leader cares to know them personally.

Celebrate.

Celebrate new risk taking
and small gain successes.
Celebrate learning from a failure. Celebrate the big stuff
and the small stuff.
Celebrate in front of everyone.
When you think you have celebrated enough,
celebrate more.
Leader champions celebrate with honesty.

Winners do not bring their boss problems, but rather enter their boss's office with three or more alternatives of how they plan to solve their problem. A leader champion is available, as a sounding board, to review your options and predicted consequences. Leader champions listen and guide solutions.

The captain of the organization ship guides the creation of the arching vision of values and a zest-filled mission that bonds and leads the shipmates. These visions and missions are the reasons for purposeful organizational existence.

Enriching the task produces decision making freedom, the possibly of exploring real challenges and real meaningfulness.

As you start to embark on new courses of action that require change, constantly ask yourself if you are still emotionally resisting the change.

Emotional ownership to changed approaches is healthy and rewarding.

Leaders Ask Questions.

Leaders constantly ask, " What can be eliminated as it is unnecessary and unwarranted, and produces time and energy wasting inefficiencies? What is needed now for a greater return on the investment of human capabilities? How can I improve my employees job satisfaction, growth, and contribution to the organization."

Change Agent.

Leaders are agents of change.
They alert the staff with warm-up pre-announcements of changes.
They take the time to involve all personnel who are to be impacted by the change.
They invest the time to gain personnel emotional acceptance before instituting the change.
They engage the stakeholders, telling them what the change means, why it is important, and asks for their input and support.
Recognizing that not everyone will embrace the change, the leader might help some of them find happiness elsewhere.

Questions Leader Champions Ask.

What are we proud of?
What makes us special?
What does not need fixing?
What are our best practices?
How effectively do we handle conflict?
What negative values or perceptions are hidden?
Where are our communication arteries clogged?

More Questions Leader Champions Ask.

What behavior is rewarded and what is punished?
What present management behaviors no longer fit?
In what corners are there 'we' versus 'them' attitude?
Where does our internal way of doing business hurt?
What policies and practices hinder our purpose?
Where are we sending mixed signals of both strategy and tactics?
What needs to be changed so that we can move from being Good to becoming Great?

Winners Love Winning Ideas and Other Winners.

As pessimism and negative thinking can have a detrimental and dampening impact on decision-makers, leaders are well advised to surround themselves with positive and realistic thinkers.

Doom and gloom personalities wear a person down to low levels.

Surround yourself with a kitchen cabinet of people who are exciting, creative, collaborative, bright and exhilarating.

Be alert to select individuals who serve as healthy testers of reality.

Neck-Stretching Leadership.

Employees who live down to expectation levels are the victims of themselves and of ineffectual leaders.
Today's leaders must create high levels of expectations for team members.
Leaders must provide tough-minded expectations that raise the performance bar to stretch goals.

Formal Presentations.

When making formal presentations,
walk in the shoes of others.
Know their needs,
their vocabulary,
their technical level,
their values,
their political climate,
their sensitivities,
their time priorities, and
their availability.
Do your homework before you present.

Motivation-Release.

Leaders manage the motivation-release from others. They do not motivate by doing things to others. The ingredients to release motivation and task ownership are:

Relationship with each employee and a differential style of leadership with each employee;

The job content and what the employee expects in his/her work life;

The degree of employee empowerment to make changes and choices in their job.

Be Careful of Pre-Judgements.

Humans make pre-judgments about others.
Prejudice is the hardening of these categories in which we see others. Everyone can be a potential winner if treated and utilized well.
Some people, initially, are disguised as potential losers, but grow and blossom into winners.

A Stable of New Ideas.

As a leader champion,
set aside time on your calendar every three to four weeks to do some hard,
exploratory thinking of new and/or different ways that your work unit could
function better.
Document your thinking in a private folder.
This readily prepares you to present those improvement ideas.
Have your stable of suggestions ready.

Invest In and For Yourself.

Severe debilitating stress can produce physical, financial, mental, familial, martial and boss relationship illnesses. When your body goes, your career goes.
Time for you will never be given to you. You must take the time to take care of yourself.

A Leadership Law is Keeping Promises.

Leaders understand that the total organization is run and held together on made commitments and promises.
The interlocking of employee to boss, employee to employee, boss to boss, and team leader to other departmental team leaders are vital to organizational excellence.
A leader's reputation and performance track record hinges on promise keeping.

Cue-Sense.

Leadership does not imply conformance, but rather a sensitivity to be alert to cues of when to change approaches as circumstance change.
A rapidly changing political climate is extremely punishing for those individuals who are not sensitive to the signals and cues in a changing organizational climate.
Sense those signs and look for cues.
Adapt.

Feelings and Logic.

Leader judgement is the combination of:
How it feels in the stomach
and the critical thinking with facts.

Listen to your stomach for cues that something just might not fit.
Then, critically analyze why you feel this way.
Be careful of acting on feelings and emotions alone because they can hardly be
logically explained, interpreted, or taught.
Yet, they are signs just the same.

Leaders are Meaning Makers.

They are weavers of zest-filled causes, beliefs in goals, and shared values.
Staff and team members search and need unifying purpose that without purpose,
results in loss of zest.
Leaders are both storytellers and honest story spinners.
The emotional buy-in and commitment based on ownership is founded on leaders
creating meaningfulness, relevance and the spirit that
we are all in it together.

Pre-Planned Escape Path, An Exit Strategy.

Leaders have a pre-planned path of escape, an escape strategy, when making
high-impact decisions.
Non-predicted downside forces can suddenly appear as progress proceeds or
stalls. Ask yourself how you can get out of the unexpected situation.
Mutual problem analysis and mutual generation of possible solutions from
relevant stakeholders can assist in answering the question of the
downside of risk taking.

Sign Language of Leadership.

Administering looks something like taking your dog on a walk, with a leash.
You have to manage the leash, control the tension of the leash to move the dog
along, sometimes even yank the leash.

Leadership, however, is more like holding a puppy in your arms, as if you are
cradling it.
You try to guide the puppy, give it comfort and support until it is ready to go on
its own.
If administering is controlling, then leading is coaching.
If administering is pushing, then leading is pulling.

Lead Like a Goose.

Geese fly in a V-shape. When the lead goose gets tired, it voluntarily retreats to another position within the V, while another goose takes the leadership position. This re-shuffling of the leadership role continues until all the geese arrive at their destination. Geese can fly many miles sharing the leadership role without concern about status or politics. What is important is the success of the entire flock of geese. Leaders are more concerned about their followership and the ultimate destination of the team than they are with personal status, recognition, or gain.

Leading Leaders

Leaders are made, not born.
They must really want the role of leading, for it often can not be fun, not glamorous, or welcomed.
Leaders are willing to overcome adversity with a clear purpose, direction, cause, and reason-to-be.
They are able to communicate this in simple terms, easily understood by others.

Leaders Are Effective and Efficient.

They know what needs to be done (effective) and are able to get others to do it very well (efficient).

By asking others how each can personally contribute to the cause, leaders develop a strong followership, inspire confidence in others and energize others with excitement, enthusiasm, and celebrations.

Favoritism.

Favoritism encourages complacency, mediocrity, and jealously.
Surround yourself with competent staff members who are loyal and will stand by you especially during times of adversity. Discourage hiring friends and family members first, who may or may not have the required skill competency.

Lead on Bad Days.

It is easy to do well when everything falls into place or when the task is easy. When obstacles arise, planned or unplanned, leaders must see it through, not blaming others or abdicating their responsibility and accountability. Complaining during the tough times makes you appear weak.

Predict the Future.

Know where you want to take the organization, your staff, and you, and how you plan to get there.
Know who will be your allies and who will oppose you.
Discover your allegiances.
Do not interfere with affairs that do not concern you for they drain your resources.
Have an exit strategy.

Losing Is Not Necessarily Losing.

The only thing worse than not meeting your goals is not having learned from
your failure.
Constantly evaluate your values, beliefs, assumptions, actions, relationships, and
consequences.
Ask what you might have done differently.

Other Oriented.

Especially during times of limited resources and stiff competition, ensure your staff has sufficient tools, time, and money to succeed.
Never spend resources on pursuits that are not valuable to your mission.
Reserve some of the resources during times of plenty for times of scarcity.
Do not place priority of your needs at the expense of your staff's needs.

Constant Feedback.

Provide feedback to your top performers who need to know what they are doing well, to maintain their edge.
Provide feedback to the weaker performers so they can improve on their performance needs.
Take immediate and decisive action to reward and punish.
If your staff achieves everything asked of them, perhaps the standards are too low. If your staff never makes mistakes, perhaps they are not trying hard enough nor taking sufficient risk.

Diagnostician.

Diagnosis (Dx) must precede intervention (Rx).
Analyze each situation to get the facts and the relationships.
Then, tailor a solution to fit the specifications.
Modify errors of judgement and execution.

Ask Questions.

Ask four times as many questions
as you provide answers.
All competence begins with a question. If you constantly provide the answers
you lose the opportunity
to increase information.

Sense of Priority.

Determine what is important and when it must be done.
Also, decide what need not be done at all.
Leaders greatest accomplishments come from concentrating on a few key areas
that make the most difference.
Do not waste time and resources that do not advance your cause, and do not
provide opportunity for growth.
You and your staff will regret and resent being misused.

Be a Pilot Not a Pawn.

Take charge of where you want to go and how you will get there.
Create a flexible plan that identifies the resources you need and the milestones
you will use to monitor your progress. Resist reacting to the immediate crisis
without pausing to reflect on its importance to your goals.
Remove barriers that prevent your from receiving real time and relevant
information. Emphasize the driving forces that facilitate real progress.

Build a Reputation as an Explorer.

Leaders visibly achieve success; build a track record of accomplishments in a specific area.

Sometimes it is necessary to go outside the traditional boundaries, like an explorer, to build a reputation.

When you are viewed as having a unique value, you no longer are viewed as a commodity.

Perceived Interdependency.

Leaders associate themselves with other leaders, help each other in times of need.
When leaders become interdependent with each other they are more inclined to
help each other.
Create interdependencies among those you can help and who can help you.
Go out of your way to help others, do favors for others, create friendships and
initiate kind gestures.

Develop Power Not Authority.

Bases of power are information, getting others involved, and asking questions and listening.
Leaders know they have power when people ask for their advice or discuss their problems with them.

Rejuvenate.

When a leader begins to feel that s/he is losing her/his edge, when the passion for leading is slipping away, it is time to rejuvenate.

Take on ordinary tasks that rebuild your confidence and show others you are willing to do the basics when needed. These ordinary tasks are probably what brought you to the level of leading you once experienced.

Celebrate your successes, and rebuild your pattern of decisive decision making.

Practical Pointers of Managing for Results.

Practical Pointers of Managing for Results.

When all is said-and-done, methods and achievements of agreed upon results are the combined bottom line. Results by any means is not the answer. People become leader champions. They are not born winners, pre-destined for the winner's circle. This Section offers practical time and priority management methods. Leader champion managers persuade, negotiate, and influence positive change in ethical ways. Some secrets of survival in the organizational political jungle include the importance of having an organizational sponsor and an ongoing relationship with a mentor to guide and protect you as you take decision-making risks. Risk-taking is the bed partner of decision making.

Time should work for you, not you for time. Are you busy with activity or are you being effective? Time is not given to you. You must take it.

Prevent on-the-job-retirement. The role of a leader champion is to provide employees with meaningful tasks to do.

A leader champion identifies what a touchdown looks like, helps facilitate others in making the touchdown, and is the score keeper, not the score maker. Leader champions manage score makers. Let the performers perform.

Perfection is the hobgoblin in a person's mind that prevents and hinders turning ideas into action. Mistakes and failures are the companions of success and leaders' judgment calls. Successful managers make more than their share of mistakes and errors because they probably make more decisions and take above average risks.

Leader champions invest in themselves by making an appointment with themselves to think. They take the time to think. Thinking time is a time to hide, not the time for an open door policy to your office. You have a right to be by yourself, to think. You will see anybody about anything, but not anytime.

Position authority is given to you from the formal job position in your organization. Personal authority, on the other hand, is never given to you. It is assumed, taken, asserted, used, and guarded as an important source of your power. Power allows you to negotiate, influence, and persuade.

You can do nothing with indecision. Decisions may or may not be final, but few will be fatal! Live with your fears and make an action decision. The perfect decision does not exist. Perfection only exists in eulogies and obituaries. Choose purposeful action rather than perfection. It is career healthier.

Be a rock and block remover to facilitate the achievements and touchdowns of others. Leader champions do not make touchdowns. They facilitate getting the organizational blocks out of the way so their staff can make the touchdowns.

Empowering staff members with authority and freedom within perimeters and parameters releases motivated commitment, and facilitates and promotes others' ownership and pride. Empowerment is a core leader champion behavior that asks people to explore and to grow. It is much more than basic delegation.
Pick your organizational battles wisely. Not everything has to be an organizational war. Not everything is worth fighting over. If it makes a difference to you, continue to fight. If you really see the issue of low priority, possibly compromise may be an answer. The ongoing relationship between you and others is key. It is Ok to back off at times.

Do not compete against your own staff to prove your technical knowledge or self-worth. They need you to collaborate and cooperate, rather than compete or show superiority over them. Walk among them to identify their issues and concerns. What do they not talk about?

A Mentor is a Gifted Guide.

More persons are pulled up the career ladder than pushed up. Career ascent is partially built on mentoring guidance, mentoring sponsorship, protection, and projecting political visibility by a mentor. Build multiple political and learning connections in the organization. Learn from the mentors by diligently asking questions and graciously listening. Without organizational visibility of your performance and that political visibility projected by sponsoring mentors, your accomplishments can translate into salary increases, but limited or no career promotions. Management excellence is a combination of political acumen and mentor guidance on how to avoid the rocks and blocks on the performance road.

Bed Partners to Managerial Risk Taking.

Decision-making is risk taking. When risk taking turns into a loss, do not lose the lesson. When mistakes are made, managers have bounce-back resiliency and ask themselves what they learned. Do not mentally play, pretend, by wearing rose colored glasses. Correct what can be corrected, acknowledge what needs to be acknowledged. Failure, hurtful errors, and criticism are the bed partners to judgment calls. Successful managers make more of their share of decision mistakes because they more decisions.

Perfect plans and decision perfection are the cast off shadows of an ineffective decision-maker as perfection hinders turning ideas into action. Nothing is done with indecision.

Mark B. Silber, Ph.D. And Antonio F. Vianna, M.M.

Flags on the Managerial Golf Course.

Presentations of new ideas can produce resistance flags on the managerial golf course of change. The resistance flags tell the manager that there is a hole or a gap between what presently exists and what is being proposed. Effective persuaders stop presenting, selling and telling, when they become aware of raised flags. Flags are opportunities to ask questions and listen to explore the holes. Are the resistance gaps based on perceived hostility to persons, cultural lore, or perceived criticism of existing beliefs?

Management is Not a Position. It is Decision and Action.

Anxiety is an enemy of a manager. The antidotes to this poison are standing up to making a decision and implementing action. After a few miss-calls in previous decision making, some managers start to hesitate and even stop making decisions. As nature abhors a vacuum, so do organizations abhor decision vacuums. If a manager stops making decisions, another rival manager moves into that vacuum and takes his/her decision making and power away. Organizational progress is based on decision making. Movement and momentum are towards committed targets.

Meet and Greet With Sincerity.

A prescription for the career death rattle is managing-by-distance. Management ineffectiveness can be caused by being a disappearing manager. This is someone who hides from the staff. Do not hide in your office. An office is a dangerous place from which to manage. The absentee manager is a person who avoids facing disagreeable persons, issues and situations, and who abdicates their leadership. Rather, be out of your office where all the ideas, problems and staff talent intersects. Walk and talk with your team members with a listening ear. Do not spend time on people, but rather invest time with people. Find out what is happening in their lives at work.

Empowerment is One of the E's of S-E-C-R-E-T-S of Success.

Strive by expecting neck-stretching objectives.
Empower employees by giving them choice freedom.
Carry a notebook. Do not trust your memory of promises.
Resolve to take decision making risk for results.
Effort focus and concentration. Clear away time clutters.
Transition from personal achieving to facilitating achievers.
Setbacks and rejections are learning opportunities.

Mark B. Silber, Ph.D. And Antonio F. Vianna, M.M.

What is Your"E.Q."?

A manager's Education Quotient increases as that person commits to regular
learning experiences and cross-training exposures.
Counting only on past education to launch you into a higher career level is a
pathway to failure.

Words and Dress.

Others in the organization, just like you, sit in judgment of how others' look and talk. Appearances make impressions that last. Dress for success. How one appropriately dresses reflect not only their present role, but also telegraphs signals and signs of future career aspirations. The quality of grooming reflects self-image and self-confidence. Language and the use of accurate and quality vocabulary directly relates to ones projected image. We are our vocabulary.

Human Relations

Human Relations

Develop trust with others, a belief that you will do what you say you will do so others can depend on you; develop harmonious working relationships with a diverse group of stakeholders.

Mark B. Silber, Ph.D. And Antonio F. Vianna, M.M.

Trust is the Glue that Makes Things Happen. As a Manager You Must Establish Trust With Your Staff, Boss, Peers, and Other Stakeholders.

When others trust you, they place confidence and faith in you without fear or misgivings. They believe you will carry out what has been agreed upon, which can be formal or informal, intentional or unintentional, acknowledged or assumed. Trust helps everyone manage his or her affairs without needless worry, anxiety, stress, or suspicion. It helps direct everyone's energies in a positive way.

Trust-worthiness does not happen accidentally or spontaneously.
It is a purposefully planned and ongoing process.
You improve your chances of being trusted when you are believable, competent, interpersonally skilled, durable, and fair.

Management is about relationships, and an investment in people for the long run, taking the good with the bad. Take the long-term perspective; avoid short-term wins.

Building and sustaining trust is ongoing. While some people are initially more trusting than others there are questions to be answered in a positive manner: Who are you? What are your intentions? This means you must take the first step in the relationship. Demonstrate you are worthy of being trusted. Others must believe in you as a person, believe you care about them as a person, and have something special to offer them that will endure over time.

The way you conduct yourself, what your appearance is, the words you use, and the alignment between what you say and what you do increases your odds of being trusted.

Packaging is important. You need to look and act the part. People judge you very quickly. Once that mind set is established, it is difficult to overcome. Speak and act in a friendly manner, non-adversarial. Encourage others to share their ideas. Positively acknowledge others point of view, especially when it differs from yours. Genuinely compliment others.

Be Sensitive to Others. Know What to Say and Know What Not to Say. Listen with Understanding and Provide Insight and Perspective from Your Point of View. This Helps Build Trust.

Each of our relationships with others has something to do with motives. What is in it for me...for you? Why are you doing this? What am I doing this? Eliminating the real and perceived appearance of hidden agendas furthers your chances of being trusted.

Establish shared values, common and agreed upon things, issues, that are important to a wide variety of stakeholders.

Managers celebrate successes, both big and small. They are interested in finding people doing good things. Be a cheerleader and a good 'miner.'

Put aside your personal agenda in order to advance the mission of the company and of your department.

Your Peers and Staff See and Hear You Through Their Stomachs and Wallets, Not Only Their Ears and Eyes.

Find ways to:
respect the dignity of others,
satisfy their needs, and
build relationships.

Managers Treat Everyone As a Customer. 'What Can I Do For You Today?'

There are no stupid questions. Anticipate what the other person wants. Allow them to be wrong on occasion. Make them feel welcome when they come to you instead of making them feel they are imposing on you. Smile. Do not mope around as if you are carrying the world on your shoulders.

Organizations Do Not Hire Unmotivated Candidates. They Become That Way By How They Are Treated and Utilized As Employees.

Explore ways to solve common and agreed upon problems that result in win-win outcomes. Be sensitive to others' needs, wants, and desires.

Interpersonal Skills

Interpersonal Skills

The core of relations is sensitivity to others' mindsets and discovering the needs of others. It is an evolving process of the growth of trust between and among persons. Trust is earned based on honesty, openness and the focused, active listening to understand others. It is sincerely being mutually interested in each other's qualities.

Have a management wedding with others, where the 'We' comes before the 'I'. Relationship sensitivity is critical to success.

Adapt a new and different Golden Rule to Do Unto Others As They Would Have Done Unto Themselves.

Never remind somebody they are a nobody or who they are not. Remind others who they are and that they are a somebody.

A leader's impact starts and succeeds with the ears, not the mouth. Ask expert questions. Stop being the person with the expert answers. Your questions make a great impact. Questioning tells others that they are more important than they think they are. Keep the focus on them, not you.

Trust can turn into rust. Manipulation hurts and harms others, and hinders relationship building. Trust is built on seeing a sign on other person that reads, "Fragile. Handle with Care."

Wisdom is the connection of the head with the heart. To lead yourself, use your head. To lead others, use your head and your heart.

Focus of Attention.

You can better relationships by focusing interest on others, rather than focusing interest on yourself. People love you when you love their interests, their concerns and issues, their talents and knowledge, their ideas and dreams. Listen to them, and then, get out of their way.

The Start and Stop of Leading.

The Start is 'I am listening', and on the trailing end is 'Well done. Thank-you.'
Subordinates' stress comes about when bosses do not listen, do not recognize
and reward, and do not appreciate and acknowledge. Undeveloped leaders
use position power for their ego trips, rather than the ego reward of their staff
members.

Ego-Swallowing.

Active listening and caring makes a bigger sound than a loud-mouth amateur. Great leader champions manage with love, not for love. Get your love at home, not at work. Catch your staff doing things right, rather than seeking to catching them doing things wrong.

Meeting New People Means Meeting Their Prejudices and Bias.

Persons have their own agendas in an interaction. It is a new interpersonal political environment to be explored and understood. To get along translates into the acquiring the skill to climb into the mindsets and values-perceptions of the other person. Be mindful of others' judgments of situations. The goal for interpersonal effectiveness is not to change the other person, but to understand where they are coming from.

Motivational Secrets.

TO BE:
give people a chance
to be themselves

TO BELONG:
people want to be
part of decision-making

TO BECOME:
facilitate their growth to
their capabilities

Mark B. Silber, Ph.D. And Antonio F. Vianna, M.M.

There is Always a Psychological Size Difference Between a Boss and a Subordinate.

The psychological size difference is the psychological space that is reduced by the leader champion when s/he raises and builds people up. Winners are not afraid of strong staff persons. In fact, they want a team of champion swimmers, not a team of non-sinkers.

Use of Humor.

Constructive and appropriate humor can be your friend in building an arching bond with others. Utilize relevant humor, but surely not humor at others' expense or humiliation. Humor heals and humors hurts. Humility facilitates. You are more of an impact than you think you are as a leader champion.

Looking into the Looking Glass.

We, the authors, are not Ministers, Priests or Rabbis. We wear our collars in the same direction as you. We teach, not preach. Whether ethical behavior is more important than ethical intent is debatable. However, we emphasize that if you do not stand for something, you just might fall for anything. Human kindness and social-moral ethics reflect in your choices, decisions, and behavior.

Nourishing Your Support Systems.

The under-whelming aspect of living and managing over-whelms us so often. Humans are hassled and the emotional bank is spent and overdrawn. We need to invest time to build up bank credits by regularly making deposits of caring to our staff and others around us.

Investing Time in Exploring the Richness of Other People is Neither Spending Time Nor Passing Time.

Active time that is regularly shared in attentive communication is vital to create an emotional support reservoir during tough times. Take time to nourish the life-sustaining strength that comes with the emotional power of your family and friends. People really care about you as you care about them. Being present in the present with people is an important secret. Stay focused with people, rather than focused on people. Being people-present is a gift. That is why we call it the present.

Success Sensitivities.

A vital idea to enrich your acceptance and to sustain and grow relationships with others is to avoid removing others' psychological make-up. People psychologically cover their flaws in many clever ways. The covering is intended to defend their perceived vulnerability and blemishes. Humanity seeks face-saving of all kinds, but especially their esteem. Accept what you can accept in others, and dare to appreciate that everyone has a blemish to some degree.

The Launching of Success is Risk-Taking.

Self-doubt and the build-up of anxiety are the enemies to those willing to take risks. The antidote to the poison of anxiety is action. Personal relationships, progress, profit and performances are forged on the anvil of risk. The successful leader champion is one who has the courage to make some mistakes. Some mistakes are final, but few are fatal. Contract with yourself to invest in some risk adventure.

Victor or Victim?

Stuff happens: setbacks, disappointments, rejections and defeats. Life is not fair. The healthy way to handle these happenings is to ask yourself, "What did I learn so I will not repeat the mistake. Next time, what will I do differently?" Some childish-people react with creative excuses to convince themselves they are victims. They become emotionally paralyzed to prevent from effectively dealing with future constructive actions. Victorious athletes know that to be a champion, they must pick themselves up and press on for self-renewal. The sting of criticism hurts, but self-revitalization attenuates the pain of failing. Leader champions stay in life's ball game.

Human Hurts and Hates.

Handling life's hurts is a solo flight of self-healing. Hurts give birth to hate and hate can arouse the anger to get even, or to balance the scales of pain. You can not get ahead by tying to get even with others. Silent grudges and bitterness will eat you up inside. Hate hurts the hater more than it hurts the hated.

Living Legacy.

Life's time does fly. Living, learning and loving quickly pass because we are preoccupied with today's issues and tomorrow's agenda. Are any of your present energies focused on giving efforts? What are your giving footprints going to be as the future looks back at your contributions? Your legacy is created only when you give of yourself so that the future of others is in a better position. Have you given today?

The "E" in Time is Effectiveness.

A salient and significant core ingredient in the mix of personal living effectiveness is the management of time. Time moves at the same speed for everyone, 60 seconds in a minute and 60 minutes in an hour. However, how we perceive and utilize time produces unequal differences among individuals. Your management of time is based on your value for time. You time value influences your time-choices.

Here are some tough-choice suggestions on personal time management:

Remove the clutter that wastes your time.
Specify each week a time to think about your goals.
Allocate 10-20% of your time to new knowledge growth.
Prioritize tonight for tomorrow: must-do from nice-to-do.
Create opportunities. Do not wait for your boss to ask or tell.
Identify where you are confusing being busy with achieving.
Think about your time availability before you make promises.

Mark B. Silber, Ph.D. And Antonio F. Vianna, M.M.

Open Dialog.

People prefer open dialog and discussions, not advice.
Mutuality does not gain with parallel monologues.
Assist in defining problems, not telling or selling.
Few people like a managerial-salesperson.

Personnel Matters

Mark B. Silber, Ph.D. And Antonio F. Vianna, M.M.

Personnel Matters

Be objective and fair, demonstrate ways to help others gain success; follow established legal and organizational protocols; encourage a positive uplifting environment.

Develop probing interviewing and coaching/counseling skills. Know the employment laws that guide the employer-employee relationship. Avoid legal liabilities. Promote a hostile free working environment.

Ensure the work environment is safe and free from hazardous and unhealthy conditions. Conduct safety audits and take immediate corrective action.

In addition to rewards, be prepared to withhold rewards and administer punishments fairly. Be consistent. The reward or punishment needs to fit the action or outcome.

Create a Backup/Succession Plan to Replace Yourself.

Identify employees who are willing and able to be your replacement. Jointly analyze their interests, competencies, motivation, and capabilities. Provide opportunities for them to excel without creating an unhealthy or antagonistic atmosphere. Offer training, rotational assignments, mentorship, and extra work assignments.

Encourage Life-long Learning Opportunities for All Employees.

Life long learning means you constantly look for opportunities to advance your knowledge, skills, and abilities. This benefits you and your company because it better prepares you for today's challenges and tomorrow's opportunities. It keeps you ahead of the game.

Be Flexible and Adaptive, While You Are Consistent and Fair.

This is not easy because there are restraining forces working against you. Examine your prior experiences and current attitudes about others. These two factors tend to influence how you perceive others today. A bad experience with and/or a negative attitude about someone creates a mind set, that, in turn, influences how you treat the other person.

Provide Immediate Feedback, Real Time, to Keep Performance on Target.

Reward good performance. Document acceptable and unacceptable performance, and all conversations. Identify metrics. Benchmark. Evaluate. Reward short-term wins that lead to long-term success.

Keep a Line-of-Sight.

Guide your staff's performance toward agreed upon objectives reminding each member the importance of their work and themselves as persons. Publicly commit to others. Be practical and realistic, with no grandiose unattainable expectations.

Clearly Differentiate Among Employees' Performance. Incentivize Others to Exceed Performance Expectations.

Ensure there is a mutual and agreed upon understanding between you and your staff about what is expected, how performance will be reviewed, how performance is to be rewarded, what specific incentives will be used, and what are the potential career possibilities. Provide ongoing feedback with the aim of motivating continuation of acceptable performance, and/or elimination of performance deficiencies. Provide incentives that are directed at the employees' needs and interests. Clearly differentiate among unacceptable, acceptable, and exceptional performance.

Goals and timetables should be challenging and realistic, clear to all relevant stakeholders, have timelines, accountabilities, and ways to assess and monitor work in progress.

Develop a recognition system to reward both individual and team contributions.

Be careful about emulating other people, departments, or companies. That which makes one successful does not guarantee it makes you successful.

Imitating others suggests there is one right way to manage. Sometimes doing what others are not doing is best.

Mark B. Silber, Ph.D. And Antonio F. Vianna, M.M.

Train. Prepare Employees for Future Assignments and Promotional Opportunities. Set High and Achievable Standards.

Identify and define specific organizational competencies that the organization requires today and requires in the future. Create training and development initiatives that are specifically directed towards developing those competencies in the employees' skill set.

Recognize the Changing Nature of the Workforce.

The workforce entering the marketplace today is different than it was ten years ago. Today's workforce wants flexible work schedules and the chance to telecommute. They prefer to work alone or as a member in cross-functional teams. Most prefer high autonomy with freedom to make independent decisions. Many are interested in part time or temporary work. These challenges become demands on the manager to be highly flexible while at the same time focusing all work towards meeting company objectives. Resolving inter- and intra-conflicts, facilitating efficient time management, and keeping all communication channels open is an imperative.

Three T's of Management.

When an employee does not perform, is it:
A selection error that calls for **Training** (coaching and counseling),

A placement error that calls for Transfer, or

A managerial decision that calls for Termination?

Thorns in the Group Garden.

Sometimes there are thorns in the group garden among the roses of achievers. Be aware of the thorns that disrupt and disturb the group and team processes. Leader champions constantly weed the garden. They prefer to have happy ex-employees rather than unhappy employees. Let people be successful, even if it means some other place.

Regular Performance Feedback.

Performance feedback is the milk of management. People want to know how they are doing and where they stand in your judgment of their performance. Do not save up praise nor save up improvement suggestions. Performance review might be every month.

Performance Stepping Stones Can Quickly Turn Into Stumbling Stones.

After you set target goals, check constantly for deviations between what was planned-predicted-desired to what is actually occurring. Catch deviations from expectations early and quickly. Stay close to the pathways of desired progress without interfering with the progress. Watch for new interventions, unplanned hitches, deviations, and unexpected behaviors. Set markers to analyze progress and deviations.

Sensitivities

Sensitivities

Be observant about how others react to you, and respect the dignity and values of others without compromising your own belief system. Stop other's behavior that undermine positive feelings and relationships.

B. A . F.

All humans are afraid at times. They are afraid of criticism and rejection of their ideas, their plans, and of themselves. Express your ideas in a manner that is neither hostile nor disrespectful. Be prepared for both praise and criticism in return. Do not allow your preconceived fear of rejection interfere in making proposals. Reorganize and rearrange Features-Advantages-Benefits to **Benefits-Advantages-Features.**

Stay Healthy.

Death is God's way of telling you to slow down. When your health goes, your career goes. When you body goes, your effectiveness and career go.

Know and honor your limits. Never attempt to promote yourself as an authority or expert in too many areas. Accept yourself without the constant need to prove yourself neither as all knowledgeable or always in control of everything.

Publish and post your department's vision and mission statements, including all employees' signatures for all to see and understand.

Keep in-tune with your company's culture, needs, and objectives. 'Company fit' is the trump card for personal success in any organization.

Reinforced Success is the Foundation for Additional Success.

Celebrate successes.
Celebrate achievements.
Celebrate learning from failures. Celebrate the risk itself when it serves to obtain accomplishment.

Study Your Boss.

Understand your boss's values, perceptions, goals, promises, commitments, pressures, motives, and work style. Some bosses listen and pay attention through their eyes. Others pay attention and learn through the written word.

Mark B. Silber, Ph.D. And Antonio F. Vianna, M.M.

Culture and Organizational Climate.

If you are political and politic, your optimal environment is a political jungle. If you are not a politically oriented person, stay away from a toxic, highly political jungle. Survival in a culture depends on quickly and accurately assessing the degree of politics played in the environment. Who is romancing you and why are they doing it? Stay away from toxic individuals.

Management Career.

There are many reasons to chose Management as a career.

None is worse than when someone else makes that decision for you.

Decide why you want to manage.
Be sensitive to your needs.

Too many people are promoted into management only because of their strong technical competence. They often fail because they are not sensitive to the other elements of total management. Some people even accept management for the wrong reasons, such as status, perks, or salary. They too often fail.

Let the Prime Reason Why You Choose Management Be To Help Others Succeed; To Be a Helper.

A manager helps advance others' successes and is willing to empower and encourage others. S/he facilitates, stays out of the way, and provides necessary support and resources.

How do you know if you are helper? Ask yourself to describe times when you helped others to succeed. How did you feel? Did you actually help?

Learn to be resourceful in expressing your diversity of talents, adaptability, and value to your company without alienating others.

Constantly learn to observe the world around you, to be aware of your environment. By expanding your awareness, you collect information to make informed decisions. When you increase your awareness you increase the quality of your choices.

Free Yourself of Clutter Which Wastes Your Time and Life.

Own your choices and your decisions. By being accountable, you gain personal control of your life.
A key to communication is to keep everyone informed. Go where they are, not where you are. Understand others' needs and wants, wishes and desires.

You increase your personal power by knowing you have choices based on the information you have collected. Choices give you options. Options help prevent you from feeling like a victim.

Hire the 'right' people the first time, even if it takes you more time than you want. Be willing to say 'no' if the candidate is not right for the company, department, relationships and job.
Know when to cut your losses. When the investment in the employee does not produce for you a net gain, take corrective action that may include transfer, demotion, remedial training, and termination. Do not jump too quickly to your decision. People's performance naturally rises and falls in cycles.

Positively express your ideas with enthusiasm and confidence without overwhelming others.

Take the initiative, rather than simply react. Gather relevant information from a variety of sources. Look for openings and opportunities.

See the World As a Creative Child As You Simultaneously Leverage Your Experiences. This is a delicate Balance, But a Proven Approach to Being Great.

Suppose you recite a poem several times until you memorize it. You might be very good at repeating verbatim the words. However, you might lose over time the true meaning of the poem because you have become too familiar with it. The key is to remember the poem's words and concurrently its true meaning. Develop others to improve their current performance and future capacity.

Patiently invest time in the workforce. Seek a balance between short term and long term employee gains.

Learn business skills in budgeting and finance. Know how to read your company's financial statements.

Express yourself decisively without arrogance or defensiveness. Back your ideas, suggestions, and insights with sound material. Engage others, not alienate.

Clearly articulate your ideas, both orally and in written format, to a wide variety of audiences, in a convincing way.

Establish, support, and perpetuate teamwork by promoting cooperative efforts and resolving conflict.

Maintain self-control. Do not be impulsive. Be self-disciplined.

Manage your stress to increase your personal health and improve your performance.

Management of Feelings.

Acknowledge the feelings of people. Try to promote positive feelings in people. Management is the management of managing feelings. When people feel good about their work, their company, their colleagues, their boss, and themselves, they tend to perform well. When people are not feeling good about these things, they tend to perform poorly; they are often distracted. A manager is sensitive to others' feelings and helps others feel good about their work and themselves.

Minimize surprises and abrupt changes. Tell it like it is, and go for closure as quickly as possible without sacrificing quality. Stop rumors as quickly as possible.

Maintain a healthy life style by exercising regularly, eating healthy foods, avoiding drug and alcohol abuse, and cultivating a spiritual view.

You Have the Capacity to Expand Beyond Your Current Competencies, Beyond Your Wildest Imaginations. It is Your Choice.

Few of us will ever reach our full potential, but also, that is Ok, as long as you try to continually improve. Reaching 100% capacity means there is no more room for growth. Further, claiming you have exceeded your capacity is also impossible. Both claims are fallacies. There is always something to improve on, and there is no way you can do more than what you are capable of doing. Your capacity is greater than what you currently believe.

Managers see patterns and trends. They are able to interpret nuances and subtleties.

Managers see the glass half full, not half empty. They see more opportunities than obstacles.

Avoid thinking and believing that your way of doing things is the best way simply because it is your way.

Ask questions to gain clarity of understanding.

Differentiate Among What People Say, What People Do, and What Their Motives Are.

Sometimes all three are aligned with each other. Many times, they are not. However, do not be misled. Substance is different from style, although one can add to or subtract from the other. Unworthy motives may or may not contaminate the information.
Make sure the information you use to form your decisions is current, not replaced by information that is more recent.

Ensure the information you use to make decisions is credible, believable, and logical.

Do not let the majority or the minority point of view be what sways your belief about something or someone.

Use information that
relates to the subject at hand. Do not be swayed by information solely because you are familiar with it.

Mark B. Silber, Ph.D. And Antonio F. Vianna, M.M.

Avoid Hasty Conclusions, Over-Generalizations, and Stereotypes. Examine Your Expectations.

Your expectations are your personal forecast of how you intend to react to a future event. A positive expectation can lead to a positive reaction, whereas a negative expectation can lead to a negative reaction. Your action, in turn, causes a reaction. That reaction becomes self-fulfilling because it reinforces your original expectation.

To Enhance Creativity and Critical Thinking, Ask 'What-If' and 'Why' Questions. Examine Your Assumptions.

Assumptions are those hidden pieces of information that we do not challenge, but take for granted as the truth. We use assumptions to make decisions. Some assumptions are Ok to use. Others are not appropriate when they are misleading or inaccurate. Assumptions are based on your feelings, experiences, attitudes, expectations, beliefs, interests, and motives.

Maintain a Diary of Your Successes and Failures. Identify Patterns. Take Corrective Action.

Perform an occasional personal time management audit to evaluate how you spend your time. Ask four questions:

What did I actually do during the past day, week, or month?

What were the specific results of my actions?

Was I satisfied with those results/ why/why not?

Was I sensitive to my needs and others' needs?

Additional Time Management Questions.

After performing a personal time management audit, ask further questions:
What did I do that really did not need to be done at all?

What did I do that could have been done by someone other than me?

What did I do that wasted other people's time?

Prioritize.

After answering the previous questions, establish the importance of tomorrow's activities:

What are the things that I must do, regardless?
What are the things I should do when time permits?
What are the things I would like to do if given the chance?
What are the things I do not have to do?

What are the things that will get done by others, or simply go away.

Then, complete those things that you must do, first. Be sensitive and tolerant of others in the process.

Managers manage projects, processes, and people. You must establish priorities, keep the work flowing smoothly, and guide people's actions concurrently.

Know the company and issues of your boss. Vertically align your staff members' individual goals with your department goals and with the company's goals.

Know what other department goals are. Horizontally align your department's goals with other departments' goals.

You are expected to work long hours, to sustain extended periods of work. Be careful not to burnout. Find ways to replenish yourself.

Walk around, talk with people, and listen to what they say.

Success: Personal Living Effectiveness

Success:Personal Living Effectiveness

The trilogy of an individual's present and future career is
job life visibility,
leadership poise, and
well being in living one's personal life.

The nerve which never relaxes-

The eye which never blanches-

The thought which never wanders-

The purpose that never wavers-

These are the masters of victory.

{Burke}

Other -Person Focused.

Personal living effectiveness starts with the ears, not the mouth. You have two ears, but only one mouth. Use them in that same ratio. You can only develop an understanding with another person as you listen to their needs, their fears and where they are hurting. By being other-person focused, by actively listening to their wishes and opinions, you can begin to build a mutual relationship.

Obstacles or Opportunities?

What you seize is what you get. Opportunity might knock only once, but it passes by the door every day. You have to keep focused on those passing opportunities so you can open the door from the inside. The door of opportunity has only one doorknob and it is on the inside of the door. Is your personal living focused on what can go wrong, or is your living focused on the moderate risk-taking of a success-seeker? Leader champions are success seekers, not failure avoiders. Which is you?

Prevent Being Your Own Worst Enemy.

Living effectiveness is not beating others at their game. It is about being oneself and controlling oneself in your own chosen and ethical ways. Do you know and follow your own life's rules and beliefs? In following others' demands of, "ought, should and must," have you become your own worst enemy? Self-control and avoiding playing life by others' pressured expectations are key to your vitality. The challenges are to know who you are, what you stand for and against, and what you want to be. Then, develop a realistic plan to get there.

Mark B. Silber, Ph.D. And Antonio F. Vianna, M.M.

Matchbook Goal-Setting.

New Year's resolutions so often fail to translate into action because there are too many of them. If you can not get your goals limited to the back of a paper matchbook, you probably have too many. The odds of a person's future do not get better just by hoping. The probability of success in the future gets better by planning. Goals give your personal living direction, purpose, and meaning in allocating your time. Set targets that are realistic in matching your time and resources. Publicly sharing your goals sustains motivation. The sharper the focus of your goal, the higher the probability you will accomplish it.

Every Choice Can Be a Good Deal.
The B:B Ratio.

Every choice is a relationship between **B**enefits and **B**others. The **B**enefits are in the numerator, such as recognition, gain, and growth. The **B**others are in the denominator, such as cost, worth the time, possible heartache, hurt, and hassle. When deciding, think through the **B:B** ratio.

C-O-M-P-E-T-E Against Yourself.

Commit to stretch and strengthen beyond present skill levels.
Objective and explicit goals with time-specific to hit targets.
Measurement of success: assess action outcomes.
Plan and anticipate step-by-step progress and predicted barriers.
Examine different ways to behave in similar situations.
Try something new, different, and unique to your living mode.
Expect to win when facing setbacks: face your fears with confidence.

Mature Coping Versus Coping-Out.

Accept yourself and others as being O.K.

Have the courage to say No, by being polite.

Develop a feeling of intimacy with loved ones.

Dare to dare. The greatest risk is to risk nothing.

Discover the importance you have to others' life.

Risk being spontaneous, enthusiastic and curious.

Trust yourself to express healthy, positive feelings.

Use appropriate humor that is uplifting, not hostile.

Savor your successes as one savors good hot soup.

Act on your ethics and beliefs when making choices.

Commit to personal growth and expansion of talents.

Be realistic with a set of expectations for your future.

Establish G-R-E-A-T Resolutions.

Goals are to be specific and measurable.

Realistic targets, not unattainable objectives to frustrate you.

Enthusiastic about your resolution because you own it, not ordered from others.

Adaptive in your approach since conditions will most likely change.

Time driven that helps you gauge your progress towards success.

Life's Dares for Personal Effectiveness.

Decide, not hide.

Let go of hostile agendas.

Be direct in handling problems.

Be modest, honest, and humble.

Celebrate your accomplishments.

Be curious, not just playing it safe.

See others differently and uniquely.

Be a dream-doer, not stopping short by just dreaming.

MoreLife's Dares for Personal Effectiveness.

Build bridges of understanding with persons new to you.

Differentiate your problems from those belonging to others.

Deal with your identified areas of self-dislike and depreciation.

Regularly audit your interest, skills, motivation, and capabilities.

Personal Occupational Satisfaction.

Disenchantment with career choices and work lives seemingly run deep. Are you doing your job because you feel you have to, not necessarily because you want to? Are your interests, skills, motivation, and capacity adequately recognized by your employer? Do you go home feeling energized, no matter how hard you work? Do you have passion and commitment for your job? Is your personal value system aligned with your professional and organizational value systems?

Practical Management Ideas.

Practical Management Ideas.

The two major objectives of management are:
P= motivational impact on PEOPLE
and
P= increasing PERFORMANCE PRODUCTIVITY.

The core component of both P's is influencing negotiated changes. Changes are facilitated when people take motivational-ownership of meaningful tasks through the utilization and growth of their talents. Productivity changes succeed as managers communicate clear targets of performance expectations based on tough-minded decision making.

Mark B. Silber, Ph.D. And Antonio F. Vianna, M.M.

The Cost Savings Calendar.

Mark your managerial calendar, every
6 months, to embark upon a semi-annual housecleaning of pockets-of-losing-
money.

The managerial question to ask is, "where can we save operating costs?"

The managerial solutions might be
where you can combine back-office operations, reduce overlapping procedures
and processes, and integrate purchases with one another.

Predict For Future Successful Operations.

To maximize the investment in your employees, forecast with your staff the skill-sets that are expected to be needed for future successful operations. Ask the following questions: What current employee skill-sets will be needed in the future? What current employee skill-sets will not be needed in the future? What employee skill-sets not needed now but will be needed in the future? Factors that influence your decision making include changing technology, globalization, employee diversity, government regulations, competition, educational level of candidates and employees, world conflicts, customer attitudes and preferences, and organizational financial capability.

Partners In Progress.

Require your vendors, suppliers, and contractors to provide free and ongoing educational and support services to your personnel. Expect and demand more in both time and services from your vendors, suppliers, and contractors. They are your partners in progress.

Employer-Union Relationships.

Continually find ways to improve your relationships with your current employer-union relationship. Work to improve communications to minimize work disruptions, anger backlash, and tension. Where possible, share in offering the union a voice in constructive changes to manage costs and invest in the workforce.

Face Conflict.

Managers must regularly, consistently, and directly face conflicts within and between operating areas. If conflicts can not be resolved, at least, work to manage and restrain them for mutual satisfaction. The goal is early detection of blocks and dysfunctional changes between operating areas. Avoiding or squashing conflict often leaves the dilemma to another day, or to another unsuspecting manager. Conflict usually grows in intensity.

Rumors.

Listen for and quickly kill false rumors. Openly share honest information to correct the punishing rumor mill. Otherwise, fear emerges within the workforce. Fear influences employee decisions to stay or remain with the organization. If they stay, in spite of fear, employee dedication, loyalty, communication, and even ethics are compromised. If they leave, the organization is left with expensive recruiting initiatives, a tarnished organizational image, and delays in work progression.

Mark B. Silber, Ph.D. And Antonio F. Vianna, M.M.

Self-Imposed and Other-Imposed Pressure.

There are two types of pressure, self-imposed and other-imposed. Manage self-imposed pressure. You have the ability to leverage this to attain peak performance. Be keenly aware of other-imposed pressure. You have less ability to manage this because it is often unpredictable and uncontrollable. However, by increasing your awareness of other-imposed pressure, you can learn from it and adapt to it.

Be Careful About Admiring Your Own Work.

Self-admiration tends to create false impressions of self-worth and reduces your belief of the need to improve. When you feel so compelled to congratulate yourself on a job well done, wait until the entire job is complete. Then ask yourself how you can improve.

Motivation.

Motivation.

One of the many tightly held secrets of leadership is how to align the employee's identification of him/herself, to his/her profession, to the job, and to the organization. How can the leader gain the employee's emotional passion and ownership of their assignments? While many leaders have insight into building team commitment, motivating the employee is something different. Leader champions encourage working with employees and by stimulating the release of their internal motivation that is already within them.

Major Molecules of Motivation.

Accept others as people who have previous successes and shortcomings. All persons have some emotional baggage from their life experiences.

The job content should encourage self-expression and facilitate degrees of individual freedom to project, somewhat, the employee's individualism.

Some persons seek high consideration and recognition from a manager. Others need high structure and order. Manage others in terms of what they expect a good boss to be.

Motivation: What Can I Really Do?

Employees are possibly suited to contribute in many places within the organization. Once the candidate is hired, the placement question is where is the optimal venue for the new employee so s/he can add valuable contributions? Put the person in a venue to find job joy and organizational value.

Motivation is not something managers do to people. It is what managers do with people based on understanding individual differences. Managers provide placement of employees to excel and contribute.

What is Your L. A. Q.?

Highly talented and strong willed employees need leadership guidance by
flexible handling.
Different people need different approaches.
And often times, the same person requires different handling.
One managerial shoe does not fit all. What is your L. A. Q.,
your Leadership Adjustment Quotient?

How Do You Say No?

'No' is one of the more difficult words to say. It produces irritation, anger, disappointment, and even sarcasm. Managers need to be tough minded. They are duty bound to reject poor proposals or costly suggestions that do not reflect value to the enterprise. They are obligated to the stakeholders to hire and promote qualified employees, while denying others that opportunity, based on their contributions or competence. The manager must develop artful yet direct and honest tactics to fulfill his/her duty as the manager.

The Higher You Ascend, The More Your Anatomy Shows.

Entering management is entering a heightened arena where possible criticism looms of whatever you do. There is little room for error, yet you will make your fair share. How you respond to the criticisms, whether politically or performance motivated, is another story. Prepare yourself for the attacks and listen to what people say. Then evaluate and adjust as needed. You will grow that way.

Implement a Manager's Chat Room.

This is not a planning meeting, a decision-making meeting, or a call to action meeting.
This meeting is where you engage in informal interactive discussions with colleagues from your industry, profession, company; city, state, national, or global wide.
You exchange ideas and build relationships.

Mark B. Silber, Ph.D. And Antonio F. Vianna, M.M.

Management By Walking Around.

Managing from behind a desk and inside of your office creates suspicion and perceptions that you do not care about what is really happening in the organization, by those who are really doing the work. These beliefs create a sense that you do not care about them, the employees. When the employees believe you do not care about them, they do not care about you. Get out of your office, and walk around. Talk with your employees, face to face.

Do Your Employees Have a Tingle?

If you want your employees to have a tingle, a feeling of excitement and interest in their job, career, you, and the company, you might consider the following:

Show them that they and the work they do are important and useful to the company.

Ask them what they want out of their job, from you, and the company.

Show them they are part of something great.

Help them be proud of the company and its products and services.

Show them you care about them as individuals.

Be Authentic.

Do not gossip or in any other way intentionally hurt another employee. If, by chance you hurt someone unintentionally, find a way to make them as whole as possible. Apologize. Admit you made a mistake, and promise not to do it again. Do not talk behind the back of others, ridicule them, or make fun of them. Whatever you do to someone behind his or her back eventually comes around to face you.

Three Terrific Motivation Thoughts.

People are willing to make the choice to release their inner motivation when they clearly understand what is expected of them, how their performance will be rewarded, and when their performance will be rewarded.

People will call to action their best performance when they have the necessary tools to get the job done, understand the sense of urgency to complete the job, and clearly recognize the problem or issue.

People tend to excel in performance when they believe there is fairness in the distribution of the rewards. There is a perceived distinction among exceptional, good, and not so good performance.

Teams.

Teams.

Leadership in the 21st Century organization highlights the significant transition from individualized performance to team achievement. Leadership of team formation and the facilitation of teaming excellence are held in higher regard than personal accomplishment.

Today's team leader facilitates the creation and subsequent focus on a common vision and mission, the supporting of interdependent relations and trust and the encouragement of honest communications across the team member's diversity. Team leadership is action, not a position.

Teams are enriched and enhanced by the leader's art and learned skills of how to select and then integrate members. Team members differ from each other in the talents they bring to the team table. They project differing degrees of emotion in proposing problem solution options. This Section presents the team leader's multi-faceted roles that call upon numerous skill sets and sensitivities.

More Sick Symptoms.

The team leader fails to ferret out and stimulate the thoughts of all team members. A few members dominate and some members do not share ideas.

Sub-goal accomplishments are not rewarded, acknowledged nor celebrated.

Cooperation breaks down and behind-the-back gossip replaces open communication. Pointing of fingers of blame and guilt to shame others produces defensive self-protection and generate excuses, not reasons.

Facilitating Team Excellence.

The group disciplines itself to stay on the tracks of progress. When discussions meander down tangential side subjects, all team members act as the group leader for re-focusing. Time is group life and group life is time.

Groups can become emotional, mixing up the search for the real problem or multi-problems that are causing the issue at hand. Excellence in problem solving is the discriminating and differentiating the symptoms from the causes of the symptoms. Problem solving starts with diagnosis.

More Facilitating Team Excellence.

Facilitating behaviors are rewarded. Responding to others' statements is handled as a dialogue, not a parallel monologue. Active listening to each other is used, rather than selling and telling to overwhelm others. Everyone seeks the common ground of understanding opposing viewpoints.

The need to dominate and the ego need for power control is controlled.

Team Wellness and Health.

Team members' defensiveness elevates when there is a perceived threat to their self-esteem, political turf, and guarded territory. Watch for signs that others in the team meeting have stopped listening. Start to ask questions.

Construct the team with persons who have inclusive values and orientations. Inclusive plays well in teams. Talk is valued by its donation, not by its duration. Inclusive team players have a desired sense of communion, embracing their self worth within a group's mission and vision. They entangle themselves with loyalty and care for others. They find pleasure in acceptance of social governance.

The Preliminary Map For The Team.

Do you know where your team is going and how it will get there?

During the forming stage of the group, identify and honestly discuss the concerns and issues of team members. What could be the boulders, hassles and the political aspects on the road of goal attainment?

Mark B. Silber, Ph.D. And Antonio F. Vianna, M.M.

Preliminary Map Continued.

Early in the team formation stage, direct the discussion of how to handle intra-team conflict and individual's deviations from performance promises.

What intra-team operational practices do you wish to emphasize as core behaviors and what debilitating practices does the team discourage?

Pre-publish the meeting's agenda. Stick to the agenda.

The After-Map For the Team.

After the meeting, compile follow through actions that will be taken by whom and when.

After every 3rd team meeting, invest time in a post game critique time to bring to light what is going well and what is beginning to operationally flounder.

Regularly take the time to look at what needs an operational sharpening.

Is the team satisfied on how it is operationally working together, or is there 'domain poisoning' of turf protection?

Signals and Signs of Team Dysfunction.

Team meetings are boring, lack a purposeful agenda, loss of leadership direction and monitoring. The difficult issues are avoided, not addressed.

Some team members feel that others are not fully committed to the group decisions. Some team members are not following through on the agreements. They are not concerned about their lack of zest for the quest.

More Team Dysfunction.

Team meetings end without specific focus on achievement targets before the next team meeting. Meeting ends without either renewed focus or agenda.

Team meetings are too quiet and peaceful with a marked absence of constructive conflict and minimal dissent. A team that goes silent hears its own death rattle. Strengthening the Team.

The ongoing attention to strengthening team excellence is both the responsibility of the group leader as well as the contributing support by and from each team member.

The leader can not strengthen the team's performance alone anymore than the football quarterback can win the game by his solo efforts.

Team strength grows when:

There is eagerness with high, yet realistic expectations.
There is freedom to explore different paths and different opportunities.
There is positive reinforcement for small, sub-step accomplishments.
There is interpersonal approval within the team.
There are honest discussions of differences between dreams and dreads.
No group member is allowed to hide.
Short-term goals are re-focused and highlighted to fit into long term goals.
Everyone honors and builds the self-confidence of each other.
Conflicts are brought out in the open, addressed and resolved.
There is shared leadership on sub-project management.
There is lots of celebration of accomplishments.

Team Success Elements:P-R-A-C-T-I-C-E

Purpose, vision and mission are clearly articulated, understood, and agreed upon by all members.

Relationships exist through collaborative processes that promote good will.

Accountability from each member of the team is evident.

Communication is ongoing.

Trust builds on interdependency.

Involvement energizes the team.

Commitment is to the zest for the quest.

Empowerment stimulates initiation of new options for implementation.

Member Selection.

Selection of team members is critical to team effectiveness, efficiency, and healthy momentum of the team's progress. Be selective who is invited into your team. Be careful what team you decide to join. Team members should be:

Fully committed to the team's vision, mission, and goals.
Willing to do what is in the best interest of the team.
Mutually accountable to each other.
Trusting of each other.
A good listener.
Collaborative.

Systems, Operations, and Structure.

Systems, Operations,and Structure.

A key to success in organizational life is the ability to scan the environment for deficiencies and efficiencies, knowing what to add, delete, tweak, and reinforce. All organizations are not created the same; each is unique, politically and structure-wise. Problems that are blamed on employees' performance deficiencies, often are, in fact, organizational obsolete systems, procedural barriers, and blocks in the system.

Change is inevitable, what we resist, persists.

Ask yourself every day how you can add value. Your goal should be to add far more value to the company than you cost.

If you are not serving the customer, you better be serving someone who is.

Stop trying to make the shoebox bigger. Design an enriching and empowering position instead.

When beginning your career in a new organization, start slowly. Listen well, and do not initially change anything. Change opportunities come in due course. Do not hurry to be the hero or heroine.

Alertness of leadership is spotting possible problems before they become an emergency or crisis.

An organization runs on promises. Keep your promises and perform those promises. Promise-making and promise-keeping builds success bridges.

You Will Never Have a Problem With People.

You will never have a problem with people, unless:

Something is changing;

Something has changed;

Someone is afraid that something will be changing.

Anxiety is the enemy of a manager.

The antidote to anxiety is attention and action.
Sub-standard performance and outcomes may not be due to the employees, but rather to outdated systems. Before you blame and shame human beings, explore how the system and processes might be the real the culprit and blocks.

When introducing change, know who the informed leader is in the group. Present the idea ahead of time to the informed group leader to iron out any forms of resistance ahead of time and to welcome his/her support. The informal leader is the person to whom others in the group come to for advice and protection. Find out what motivates the group and what the group fears. Be forearmed and forewarned.
Celebrate success and reward employees for embracing change.

Strive to meet or exceed expectations. Never say yes, when you are unable or unsure about your ability to deliver. It is your job to inform, and when necessary, reform expectations.

Reward proactive self-correction. Employees should trust you enough to tell you what has gone wrong. Understand that everyone makes mistakes. Reward employees for bringing their errors to your attention. Encourage them to propose a solution. Empower them by allowing them to implement corrective actions. Support them in sharing their experience with others. No shame and no blame.

To a manager, the words, "We have always done it that way," should be analogous to a red flag being waved in front of a bull.

Get organized. Managers can easily get lost with and in 'non-issues' of non-consequence. If you accept responsibility for a task, schedule a time to complete the task on your calendar. Do not over commit your time with busy work. Put first things first. Many managers find themselves working excessive hours to keep up with what they refer to as their real job.

Employees are not great mind readers. You better be sure to communicate your expectations clearly.

Mark it on Your Calendar.

The three and six month self-assessment dates.
Take out your last employment evaluation and your current year goals. Realign your work and your behavior to ensure you are meeting or exceeding your goals. If your plate has filled up, and your focus has been shifted, proactively address this with your supervisor to ensure you have buy-in.
If you have consensus, work with your supervisor to rewrite and adjust your current year's goals.
Failure to follow through on this step can be performance and career suicide.

Adjust the Golden Rule.

What makes you think
others want
the same things
you want?

Take the time
to understand
what other people want
done unto them.

Secret of Job Security.

Do you want to know the secret about job security?
Approach your job as if you were in business for yourself.
Approach your area of responsibility with passion and commitment to excellence.
Focus on the core and critical tasks and hold yourself accountable for those outcomes.

Sick Symptoms of an Unhealthy Team Climate.

Searching for the perfect problem solution. A fearful need for absolute certainty with the lack of decision finality and not moving on to other issues.

Agreements are made too quickly without adequate discussion. The consensus is on the solution without first exploring the possibility of multiple causes of the problem.

Do Not Throw Good Money After Bad.

When you a mistake, analyze the situation.
What went wrong?
Why did it happen?
Identify the cause(s):
Bad process
Lack of training
Lack of accountability
Who was involved?
Did anyone take ownership?
Was anyone aware of the problem?
Was the problem reported?
Was anything done to address it?
When did it happen, and did it happen more than once?
How can I prevent this from happening again?

The '24' Recipe for Managing Employee Relations.

When you are pleased, take at least 24 seconds to find the right words to praise others. Praising a job well done and acknowledging employees can not wait. Respond with a sense of urgency and enthusiasm.

When you are angry, write down your thoughts and put them in a sealed envelope addressed to yourself. Wait for 24 hours, then reread your message. See if the message is written in a manner will provide a positive outcome. If not, try writing a new message with the intent of finding a win-win solution. When we are angry, we often attack the people we need to work with, destroying trust and motivation.

Change is life and life is change. Predict it. Roll with it. Design it.

Manage the process, lead the people.

Know your team. Help them to build their jobs around their skills and the needs of the department.

Everyone wants to succeed and be appreciated. Set up people to succeed and be recognized.

Be enthusiastic in your job. Does this word describe you?

Reward what you want repeated.

Focus your energy on building a sustainable infrastructure in your department.

Train, train, or train-wreck.

Develop and enhance your most valuable assets, your employees.

As a manager, you cannot do it alone. However, you alone are responsible for the outcome.

Before Starting Any Task.

Challenge yourself and your employees to ask these questions before the start of any task:

Why am I doing this?
Is this task necessary?
Is this the best way to do this?
How does my work affect others?
Is this the right task to be focusing on right now?
Am I being efficient or effective right now?
It is always time to reevaluate the process and/or your priorities.

The focus as a manager is to recognize which projects are most important to the organization, not which projects are most important to you.

Give others what they want, not what you want.

Every time you commit the organization's resources, ask yourself if you would be willing to make this commitment if it was coming out of your pocket. Ultimately, it is.

Assess your skills through self-examination and inquiry. Solicit feedback from your staff, your peers, and your manager. Every day, seek out ways to improve and enhance your contribution to your company.

Build some depth on your bench. Surround yourself with superior performers who are filled with zest to win.

If you can imagine it, you just might be able to create it.

Know where your team members are on their career path. Over time, an individual's goals and contributions to the workforce change. In the early stages of one's career, we search for career anchors that help us define what path to take. In the middle stages of one's career, we focus on development and growth. In the late stages of one's career, we begin succession planning.

Define success for you. Then built a bridge from where you are today to where you want to be. Align your daily choices with your personalized vision of success.

Organizational Belonging and Job Ownership.

Organizational belonging and job ownership is a strong desire for most people. It represents their personalized expression of who they are. Change threatens their life space and the fear of loss or abandonment produces resistance. Involve staff in the need, design, and implementation of the changes that will affect them. A surprised staff is the adversary of management. Dialogue and open discussions, rather than surprise announcements, facilitate change acceptance.

Alignment Always.

Successful organizations develop policies, procedures and action behaviors that are strategically aligned with their vision. These polices, procedures and action behaviors create the organizations operational framework. Effective managers align themselves with the organization's vision and incorporate the policies, procedures, and action behaviors within their department.

Safe or Not? That is the Question.

Is this a safe place to make mistakes? Employees need to know if their organization considers mistakes opportunities, or grounds for dismissal. Leader champions make it safe for employees to express their opinions and to offer suggestions that are outside of the box.

Corporate Culture.

Look before you leap. Before you consider an employment offer from any organization, you should take time understand their corporate culture. Consider how your management style would fit into this organization. Why do managers leave? What was their management style, and how did staff feel about them? How long were they with the company? Try to understand what challenges you would face, and if you feel well suited for this position.

Roadmap For Success.

Create a roadmap for success.
If you want to reach your destination, take the time to document how you and your team will get there.
You will need clear and focused directions, milestones, and metrics. Estimated time in route, and of course alternate routes, in case of emergency.

Organizational Blueprint For Success.

Not all organizations are created equal. There is no one-size fits all, a blueprint for success.
To survive, every organization must be able to respond effectively to customer demands and have a unique competitive advantage.
As a leader champion, seek out an organization that has a blueprint for success that strategically aligns with your own unique competitive advantage.
Know yourself.

Tell Your Story.

Effective managers are great communicators.
They know how and when to share information. They understand their audience.
Learning how to tell your story to elicit the response you are looking for requires skill and planning.
Before you deliver good or bad news, ask yourself what message you want your audience to receive and what your desired outcomes are.
Be sure your story supports your desired results.

Buy-In.

Invest time to make sure you have
buy-in.
People accept responsibility for work assigned to them when they feel that they
have been involved in the decision making process.
Do you know when people have bought into the plan?

Feedback Above All.

Solicit and provide direct feedback.
Goal attainment is a process, not a single event.
You must manage the process, and lead the people.
Set measurable milestones that enable you to monitor progress and provide you
with opportunities to solicit progress reports and feedback.

Do You Fit?

You bring yourself to the office every day.
Your personal beliefs and values guide your decisions and actions in all aspects
of your daily life.
How well you contribute to your organizations is based, in part, on how well
your values and beliefs fit within the organization to which you are acculturating.

Diversity, Respect, Dignity.

Diversity in the workplace
is the norm.
Ethnic jokes,
stereotypes, and
prejudice
have no place
in the organization.

It Is Not Really Funny.

It is funny,
really,
that many of the same things
that got us in trouble as kids,
still get us in trouble as adults,
and for some strange reason,
that seems to surprise some people.

Life Long Learning.

Educate yourself.
Keep up to date on what is going on your industry.
Attend tradeshows, read industry literature, research what your competitors are doing.
Keep informed.

Low Maintenance, High Performer.

Strive to be a low maintenance
leader champion.

Add value to your company.

Manage your department like a well-run service center.

It should be a pleasure for your internal and external customers to do business
with you.

Balance Is The Key.

Live a balanced life.
It is not all about work.
Love, live, and enjoy life.
There are only twenty-four hours in a day, seven days in a week, and a limited number of days to live.
Remember, none of us is getting out of this alive.
Enjoy and participate.

Your Comfortable Contribution Style.

Some organizations require employees to work together as team, while other organizations require employees to work with individualized autonomy. If you want to be successful, be sure to work for a company that best suits your personal contribution style.

Risk and Reward.

Managing a career is a lot like investing in the stock market.
The greater the risk, the greater the potential return or loss.
What is your comfort level for risk?

Relevant Answers Come From Relevant Questions

A leader champion, regardless of his/her formal role or position in the organization, constantly asks questions. The questions are intended to challenge the status quo in terms of who is doing what and why, and how can it be improved. Relevant questions lead to relevant answers. Our top twenty-five relevant operational questions are listed below, albeit no special order. There are more, certainly. What would you add to this list?

1. How can our department be more internally collaborative, and with others, to reduce development time of an idea to a product or service?

2. How can we automate, delegate, and in other ways streamline our approval processes?

3. How can we save financial and non-financial resources on travel and meetings?

4. How can we increase brainstorming time with others to increase the free flow of ideas?

5. How can we gain real-time connections with our suppliers, vendors, and contractors?

6. How can we make it easier for others to do business with us?

7. How can we replace our inventory with just-in-time or print-on-demand processes?

8. How can we encourage others to reduce turf protection and isolationist activities?

9. How can we better assess and monitor customer orders to correct problems or mistakes that unintentionally occur?

10. How can we improve our business intelligence security and early warning alert processes?

11. How can we accelerate, without compromising quality and ethics, changes in our systems and operations?

12. How can we simultaneously track purchases from multiple suppliers?

13. How can we increase employee retention?

14. How can we reduce personal-identity theft?

15. How can we better forecast customer needs and wants?

16. How can we better anticipate technological interruptions, and take advantage of technological innovations?

17. How can we save our trees by eliminating unnecessary paper?

18. How can we increase our organizational capabilities and deliverables while balancing the need for additional resources?

19. How can we best develop our internal human resources?

20. How can we provide ongoing learning opportunities for our internal human resources through technology?

21. How can we improve the probability that the *right* customer receives the *right* product at the *right* time at the *right* price at the right *cost*?

22. How can we empower others to take charge and ownership of projects?

23. How can we facilitate others to think and act like an owner of the organization?

24.   How do we know if others have the necessary information and tools to do their job?

25.   How can we more effectively and efficiently process information to make better action decisions?

A Managerial Self-Awareness Tool

Among the several factors that influences managerial success is the ability to simultaneously maximize effectiveness and efficiency. When a manager is effective, s/he has identified what needs to be done, i.e., the right things. When a manager is efficient, s/he has performed in the best way possible, i.e., done things right. A great manager is able to be both effective and efficient.

Listed below are forty (40) statements. After you read each statement carefully, decide if the statement <u>Most Often</u> or <u>Least Often</u> describes your behavior. No ties.

Statement	Most Often	Least Often
I expect others to perform tasks the way they think is best.		
I expect others to get the right things done, rather than be busy and do everything right.		
I reward others for taking the initiative to make things happen, in ways that they are comfortable with.		
I delegate to others what they need to do.		
I support those who take risks, work outside of their comfort zone.		

I regularly give oral/written assignment for others to accomplish.		
I coach others to be the best they can be, in their own way.		
I focus most of my time on what needs to be done first.		
I mentor staffs who are really trying to do the best they can in their own way.		
I seek commitment from others about what they are going to do before they start doing it.		
I collaborate with others to discuss the best approach to solving problems.		
In a dispute, I listen to both sides before I make the final decision.		
I encourage others to challenge the status quo in how we do things.		
I set up specific progress review dates to review work in progress.		
I am sensitive to the unique needs and differences of others.		
I regularly review and recommend eliminating marginal projects or processes that clutter my plate.		
I ask members of my staff to alternately manage our staff meetings in ways that they think is best.		
My staff knows what tasks I expect them to accomplish.		

I am open to new ideas of satisfying customer service problems, and operational challenges.		
I reward my staff for focusing on the important tasks.		
I reward others for doing their own thinking and making their own choices.		
I concentrate on what is needed for the present and for the future.		
I avoid forcing everyone to do as I do, the way I want it done.		
I regularly assess and monitor tasks to make sure we are contributing to the company objectives.		
I concentrate on helping people explore their unique strengths and style, to find their own best approach.		
I often ask questions rather than give answers.		
I mutually explore with employees how they can enrich their own jobs, to make it more meaningful to them, to conduct themselves in their own ways.		
I focus on projects that have the chance of the greatest impact on the organization.		
I lead as a follower.		
I tell others what they need to improve on.		
I know that leadership takes on many styles, that process is important to success.		
I lead by exception.		

I encourage others to be life long learners in ways that are best for them.		
I regularly re-prioritize my staff's work.		
There are many ways to slice a carrot.		
I consistently present and assertively represent new ideas to my staff and to senior management.		
I enjoy exploring alternative ways of doing things.		
I plan each day's work the night before.		
I seek out organizations whose culture allows for learning through selective failure.		
My boss counts on me to get what s/he needs done, on time, and within budget.		

There is no universal ideal score. Periodically, review your responses to reflect if your behavior is getting you what you want. What behaviors might you strengthen, add, delete, or adjust? What commitment to change might you consider? How will you know when you have succeeded?

**My observations and notes from the above
Managerial Self-Awareness Tool:**

The Case of the Organizational Misfit

George Marshall was a recent graduate from a nationally recognized university in the Midwest. He dutifully worked full time as he pursed his Masters of Business Administration, expecting to be highly rewarded by his employer at that time for the accomplishment and hard work. George was sadly mistaken when he asked his boss after graduation, "Now that I have my Masters, what are the company plans for me? You know, the big promotion, with the perquisites and salary increase? Hey, you paid the full bill."

George's boss looked him straight in the eye to say, "What are you talking about? We never promised you anything. We are happy you earned the M. B. A. Our investment in you, by paying for the full fare, has returned nicely during the time. However, no, there is nothing planned for you. Wait your turn."

After recovering from being startled, even a little peeved, George set out to get that big job, whatever it was, whereever it was, and whatever it took. He would show 'them' how deserving he was!

Soon thereafter, he interviewed for a Vice President and Officer position at a prestigious company. They treated him royally during the interview. Two days of interviews with the executive staff and potential peers followed. He felt on top, yet he grew suspicious after the first day of interviews. He sensed inconsistencies among several interviewers. The contradictions seemed to have some negativity associated with them as well. For example, when he interviewed with his potential boss he was told that he would have complete control over the entire department, needing approval from the boss only for exceptions. Yet, when he interviewed with a potential peer, someone who also reported to the same boss, she indicated that the boss was a micro-manager, allowing little room for discretionary judgement calls. Another example occurred when the field operations personnel accused the corporate office personnel of misrepresenting facts about the financial health of the company. George simply listened to these claims, not challenging at any point during the interview process, or trying to pursue the real truth behind the statements.

After two days of interviewing ended, George's potential boss told him to seriously think about joining them. He had talked with the other executive members and they were impressed with him. George left the interview feeling very positive, putting aside his suspicions and even some of his dislikes for a few of the executive team members. George convinced himself these issues were not really important.

Two days later, George received a telephone call from the executive search consultant who offered George the job explaining that George was the most qualified candidate he had found from the nationwide search. The total compensation package was discussed, and George accepted, being assured a written offer letter and contract would follow. The formal offer letter with contract followed within two days, and George formally accepted.

A big job with a fancy title, officer position, big salary with bonus, and all the other perks. He was delighted. He knew someone would eventually understand the value he would bring to an organization, even if it meant a relocation to a place where he knew no one.

George gave notice to his employer whom conscientiously and earnestly challenged his decision. Not that he was not qualified, but did he really know what he was getting himself into. Was he doing the right thing for the right reasons? Of course, he was, he quickly answered them, albeit somewhat cautiously to himself, not fully appreciating his lack of critical thinking, being tugged along to the decision by a series of false assumptions and fallacies. The company offered him well wishes, and said he could return to the company at any time if things did not work out.

George told his friends the good news, and to his surprise, several challenged his decision. For example, did George really believe that there were no other suitable candidates in the immediate metropolitan area where the company's home office was located? What might be some of the reasons for the inconsistencies George sensed during the interview process? What about the anger and lack of respect he heard from the field operations personnel? Did George have an exit strategy in case there were unexpected disappointments? Why did not George have the opportunity to talk with his future staff? Why did the company want George to start within two weeks?

George dismissed these questions as ancillary to the job.

Thirty days into the new job he knew he had made a mistake, yet would not admit it. He found that two of his six direct reports were on probation, while the third member was retiring in two months. The field personnel lacked respect for his department, and for his boss. Unknown to George, the position he now held had been filled with an employee for fifteen years who had eventually retired, and then within three years thereafter three people were hired and subsequently fired. The company was in financial trouble, needing to bring in revenues fast or else face liquidation. The parent company began exercising its authority over the company, often contracting local decisions. George's boss made side deals with other executives that contradicted the agreements George thought he had made with them, yet his boss did not disclose the side deals to George. George's boss was only promoted six months prior, having failed miserably in a line job in the field. George's peers privately complained of similar situations yet no one would come forth openly with their concerns.

George had to save face. To no one, including to himself, would he admit he had erred. He worked harder and harder, believing he could change the culture of the organization. He substituted long hours of work for social support. He felt alone, many times. He exercised his technical, academic, interpersonal, and administrative skills. Yet, he knew this was not the place for him. Again, he believed he could change the way the organization was being run. He could get to his boss, to change him. Hey, he was a Vice President and Officer. The company must have known who he was or else they would not have offered him the job in the first place! They must have known he considered himself the chief change agent for the company! Didn't they want to change themselves?

There were many situations when his values, approaches, and techniques clashed with how things were being done in this company. Three years later, George was fired, although his personnel file indicated something such as he had philosophical differences in how the Department should contribute to the business. Being fired was the best thing that could have happened to him! Several other peers, also, were dismissed at about the same time, accused of "not signing on board."

Discussion Questions:
What might George have done to improve his chances of success?

What might George have done to improve his decision making?

What might George do now to prevent the situation from happening again?

Reflections by the Authors:

The two authors stress the importance of examining one's personal value system, what one stands for, and how one operates. George needs to critically challenge his reasoning for making decisions, to examine assumptions and beliefs. For example, if the answer is already decided, then any reason justifies it! In his case, George's answer was that he was deserving of a Vice President/Officer position, and therefore, any organization that offered it would get his acceptance.

He dismissed the importance of organizational culture; the ways things are done. He believed he could adapt and adjust as needed, to put aside his core values if necessary. He believed he could actually change the organization's value system, its culture, and his boss. He was wrong. Even if George knew others would ally with him in sharing his concerns, why did they only do this secretly, unwilling to admit their concerns openly to the organization.

Today, he must skeptically challenge most things, including himself. Not as a way to second-guess others or him, but to ask the important questions, not settling for ambiguous answers. He must be able to clearly articulate to himself and to others what his core values are and what he is not willing to change. He must become more sensitive to the nuances, what is not said, and the alignment between what people say they do/will do and what they actually do/have done. He needs to look for patterns and consistency.

Thinking critically will actually free up George from the constraints of uncertainty, and from being caught off guard or embarrassed. When he critically thinks, he is prepared to gain clarity on issues by asking questions such as "Can you tell me more about that. I do not quite understand." He must be prepared to discover the truth, even if it hurts, by asking questions such as, " How can we verify that? Why did that happen? Who said that?" He must look for greater precision by asking something such as, "Do you have more details that might help me understand what you are saying?" He must constantly wonder if the information he gains is relevant, and so he should ask, "I do not understand the connection. Could you help me by restating it another way." He needs to be as thorough as practical, so he might ask, "Did we cover everything? Have we left something out? Is there something missing that we should know about?" And lastly, he needs to be logical, so he might ask, "How does that follow from what you just said? I am not able to follow the reasoning. This does not make sense to me. Can you explain it?"

Therefore, overall, George must attempt to understand what the real issue is, what the real evidence is that relates to the issue, and then, what is the most logical conclusion he can draw from the evidence. Understanding the importance of the organization's culture, the maze we go through, to get as much cheese as possible and to avoid the shocks must be on the front burner. He must explore the subtle things such as what the organization stands for, and look for things such as but not limited to history, symbols, language, material objects, status, titles, education, slogans, dress code. George must look to see if the subtle things support the obvious things, such as the company written policies, training programs, salary structure, reward and recognition programs, and benefits program.

George must respect the value of an organization's culture, and know how difficult it is to change it.

Mark B. Silber, Ph.D. And Antonio F. Vianna, M.M.

Are You a Promotable or a Pass-Over?

Abstract

In this article, we want to talk with you about increasing your odds of promotion. This simply means increasing the odds, not being one hundred percent sure. Our collective experiences tell us that you need to have Politic Sense, Cue Sense, Boss Sense, Ego Control Sense, Servant Sense, and Career Sense. Our belief is that you can be pretty much anything you want to be, within reason. The challenges are to know who you are now, what you want to be, who can help you as well as hinder you, how you can get where you want to be, and how will you know it when you arrive. Sounds complex, but actually, it is not. It takes much of what we have already discussed in this book.

Politic Sense

When in a highly dangerous organizational political jungle, are you politically effective? Do you know the unwritten rules and the power-players, the wheelers and dealers? Do you know what is not said? When you are in an open, trusting, self-disclosing and non-political culture, these issues are less important because everything is out in the open. Do not be fooled. Very few places are not political. It is only a matter of degree.

Being politic is being aware of what is reality in others' values, what is acceptable, what will fly at any point in time with key people, and what is financially possible. You get the idea. Being politic means, you have figured out the maze of organizational life. You know where the shocks are and where the cheese is. Therefore, in other words, it is the art and craft of the possible. Knowing when the timing is right with the right people to ask the right questions is what it is all about, says the politic savvy person.

Do not misunderstand us. We are not saying that the politic person is a bad person, or does evil things. No. The politic person knows the ins and outs of the informal organization. S/he can see through the fog and into the darkness, and has a better sense of smell and feel, which leads us to Cue Sense.

Cue Sense

Do you pick up and sense the cues in your organization. Verbal and non-verbal signals are send on a regular basis, all the time, in your organization. Some of them are clear and focused. Others are vague, mixed, confusing, and contradictory. You need to scan the environment for these signals, especially being sensitive to the contractions between verbal and non-verbal cues. If you do not, it could limit your promotability or employability. Consider George in the Case of the Organizational Misfit.

Some organizations, and certainly some people, are committed to low risk or no risk decisions. Rules, past practices, and commitment to conformity is their safe way to endure, to make decisions. These people often dismiss the cues. Since the challenge of change produces insecurity and uncertainty, the individuals described above focus on the downside of danger, the obstacles. They negate and avoid negotiated confrontation. Sometimes, they focus on the downside so much that they become incapable of seeing the upside. They miss out. Their blinders are on.

The person who notices the real way things are done in the organization is sensitive to the cues. S/he watches those who are successful; what they say, how they dress, who they associate with, what battles they fight, etc..

In the end, it is always your choice to embrace the cues or to discard them. However, at least, recognize them for what they are; signals to success in your organization.

Boss Sense

There are many different types of bosses, the good ones and the terrible ones. We have discussed in this book examples of each, and the consequences of their beliefs and actions. Regardless of what type of boss you report to, you must understand that person very well.

Boss sense calls for interpersonal and psychological awareness of the needs, greeds, and fears of that person. How much emotional space divides you and your boss? What form of communication is expected from your boss? What does the boss want to hear and not want to hear? Does your boss trust you will do the right thing, be ethical, and be honest? Is your boss threatened by you and your contributions, and what you stand for? Does you boss encourage you to stretch beyond your current assignments, accept limited failures as a part of life long learning, and, in general, want you to succeed? Is your boss your mentor, confidant, helper? Is your boss approachable? Do you trust that person to do the right thing on your behalf?

Ego Control Sense

Organizational research reflects that promotable people have a health ego, self-esteem and positive self-regard. Pitfalls, however, cover the landscape when one's ego gets out of control. In the organizational marriage that you agreed to by accepting employment with your company, 'We' comes before 'Me.'

Ego sense is the healthy alertness to call upon the expertise of others, and the humility to acknowledge that you just might not have all the answers or the expertise. You need to be open and accepting of others, especially when those ideas and tactics are different from yours.

Living in an organizational setting implies reciprocity among all members. Reciprocity is hurt, hindered, and even made helpless when persons become know-it-alls and demand only center stage relationships. Healthy ego sense is relatively free from being threatened by others.

Servant Sense

The traditional view of organizational structure is pyramidal. This means the top dog is at the top, and there is only one top dog per organizational unit. Everyone else is subservient , as in underlings. Being above others implies being superior and smarter than the worker-bees.

Being a servant leader is quite different. The servant leader works for his/her staff at the same time being the formal leader. The servant leader actually wears two hats. One is the formal traditional boss who has the power of position, and the other hat is the colleague who facilitates, leads, educates, helps, guides, listens, and empowers. The servant leader keeps these two roles separate and clearly makes it clear to the staff which role is which.

To the servant leader, everybody is his/her boss. Everybody is the customer. Everybody has something to tell. The servant leader listens to all of them, and willingly incorporates appropriate ideas and suggestions, with appropriate rewards and recognition.

Career Sense

Career promotions often come faster than career demise. Career demise often is signaled by not being invited to meetings, or your name and distribution being left off memos. Eventually, you no longer fit into the organizational culture. It has passed you while you were sleeping in your office. The junior person who you trained is now your boss, and the assignments are of the complexity you encountered when you first started your career.

When you first stated your career, the song was, Who Are You? Then, it became, I Want You? Then, it followed with, Give Me More Like You. Finally, it returned to, Who Are You?

To stay on top of your career here is what you need to do. First, identify what your interests are. Successful people do what interests them. Secondly, identify what your skills are. This makes sense because you need a tool kit of skills to do the tasks assigned. Thirdly, identify what your motivation is. What turns you on and what turns you off? Fourthly, identify what your capacity is. What more can you do, and what else can you do? Fifthly, identify the best organizational fit. Where do your interests, skills, motivation, and capabilities best match? Find out more about this topic in Career Management and Employee Portfolio Tool Kit, ISBN: 1-4107-1100-5.

In today's organizational world, it makes great career sense to seek out a career mentor to support you, guide you, and encourage you. A career mentor is anyone who is honest with you about your blind spots and offers suggestions for improvement.

Leader Champion Action Plan

The real value of this practical book is the degree to which you apply these ideas. As business practitioners and educators, we suggest you read *Leader Champions* a second time. However, during the second-read, use the following page titled *NOTES* to document those ideas most helpful to you.

Then, using those documented notes, create a *Leader Champion Action Plan*. The page titled *Leader Champion Action Plan*, following *NOTES*, might be helpful in planning, organizing, implementing, and tracking your *Plan*.

When you create your personal *Leader Champion Action Plan* consider the following definition of *Key Leader Champion Resolution*. Your *Key Leader Champion Resolution* is essentially a formal expression of your intent to improve yourself in the arena of leader-champion beliefs, attitudes, behaviors, and results. A *Resolution* contains several essential elements. Using the acronym GREAT, the essential elements are:

Goal.
Your *Resolution* should be goal directed, measurable, and specific.

Realistic.
Your *Resolution* should be realistic and attainable. Lofty resolutions that cannot be
accomplished lead to frustration, anxiety, and failure.

Enthusiastic.

You should be enthusiastic about your *Resolution*. In fact, passionate about the *Resolution* itself, and in achieving it. The *Resolution* should be yours, not someone else's. You must own it, believe in it, and want it.

Adaptable.
You should be adaptable, flexible when unexpected changes occur, and they will. You might also need to adjust your *Resolution* when conditions unequivocally call for it.

Time Driven.
Your *Resolution* should contain a timeline of when you intend to accomplish it. Sub- timelines are also helpful when your *Resolution* timeline is more than one month.

NOTES

Key Points:

Current Beliefs, Attitudes, Behaviors, and/or Results I want to reinforce, to continue:

New Beliefs, Attitudes and Behaviors I want to add to my tool kit:

Current Beliefs, Attitudes and Behaviors I want to delete from my tool kit:

Current Beliefs, Attitudes and Behaviors I want to adjust for my tool kit:

Leader Champion Action Plan

Leader Champion Resolution:

I know I have achieved my Resolution when the following occurs:

Sequence of Steps	Resources Needed	Timeline
1.		
2.		
3.		
4.		
(Use additional pages if needed)		

About The Authors

Dr. Mark Silber is President, MARK SILBER ASSOCIATES, international Organization Psychology consulting firm, San Diego, Ca., founded in 1971. As one of the "Deans of American Management", Mark has also taught for 43 years in Graduate School of Business's at Loyola University of Chicago, University of California, the Executive-in-Residence at United States International University and now at the University of Phoenix.

His ten years of corporate experience was as the Management Psychologist for Lockheed (LMSC), Corporate Director of Management Development for UNIVAC and The Upjohn Company. Prior to serving as a combat flying officer in the Strategic Air Command, he merited his undergraduate degree from the University of Wisconsin. Mark's Masters and Doctorate degrees are from The Ohio State University. He is the Senior Author of two best selling books and over 140 professional articles in national journals. Worldwide, as a popular management educator and as a hands-on consultant, Dr. Silber has spoken to over 1.5 million persons in company and convention audiences.

Antonio F. Vianna is best recognized as a Human Resources Executive with over 30 years business experience helping organizations maximize the potential of their employees. He holds a Bachelor of Science Degree in Biology from Union College (Schenectady, New York), a Masters of Management from Northwestern University (Evanston, Illinois), and an Officer Commission in the United States Air Force.

He is the author of several management articles for trade magazines. He is frequently interviewed on radio and television on the topic of taking charge of your career. While still involved in Human Resources consulting, and teaching business and management courses at the University of Phoenix, he writes fiction and non-fiction. His current publications are: Career Management and Employee Portfolio Tool Kit (two workbooks to help take charge of your career), The In-ter-view (mystery novel), A Tale from a Ghost Dance (mystery novel), and Talking Rain (murder mystery).

www.ingramcontent.com/pod-product-compliance
Lightning Source LLC
Chambersburg PA
CBHW031838170526
45157CB00001B/342